Proceedings of the

19th International Congress of Classical Archaeology

Volume 50: The Rural Foundations of The Roman Economy

Proceedings of the
19th International Congress of Classical Archaeology

Cologne/Bonn, 22 – 26 May 2018
Archaeology and Economy in the Ancient World

Edited by

Martin Bentz and Michael Heinzelmann

Volume 50

ICCA
XIX
AIAC

Edited by

Peter Attema – Günther Schörner

The Rural Foundations of The Roman Economy. New Approaches to Rome's Ancient Countryside from the Archaic to the Early Imperial Period

Panel 11.1

Propylaeum
SPECIALIZED INFORMATION
SERVICE CLASSICS

Bibliographic information published by the Deutsche Nationalbibliothek:
The Deutsche Nationalbibliothek lists this publication in the Deutsche Nationalbibliografie; detailed bibliographic data are available on the Internet at http://dnb.dnb.de.

Propylaeum
SPECIALIZED INFORMATION SERVICE CLASSICS

Published at Propylaeum,
Heidelberg University Library 2022.

This publication is freely available under https://www.propylaeum.de (Open Access).
urn: urn:nbn:de:bsz:16-propylaeum-ebook-930-8
DOI: https://doi.org/10.11588/propylaeum.930

Editorial Coordination: Florian Birkner, Ina Borkenstein, Christian Schöne
Editorial Staff: Stefanie Herten, Mark Locicero

Cover illustration: Farmer preparing his Grain Field with traditional Plough (photo Peter Attema)

ISBN: 978-3-96929-100-9
e-ISBN: 978-3-96929-099-6

Universität zu Köln
UNIVERSITÄT BONN

CONTENTS

PREFACE

On behalf of the 'Associazione Internazionale di Archeologia Classica (AIAC)' the 19th International Congress for Classical Archaeology took place in Cologne and Bonn from 22 to 26 May 2018. It was jointly organized by the two Archaeological Institutes of the Universities of Cologne and Bonn, and the primary theme of the congress was 'Archaeology and Economy in the Ancient World'. In fact, economic aspects permeate all areas of public and private life in ancient societies, whether in urban development, religion, art, housing, or in death.

Research on ancient economies has long played a significant role in ancient history. Increasingly in the last decades, awareness has grown in archaeology that the material culture of ancient societies offers excellent opportunities for studying the structure, performance, and dynamics of ancient economic systems and economic processes. Therefore, the main objective of this congress was to understand economy as a central element of classical societies and to analyze its interaction with ecological, political, social, religious, and cultural factors. The theme of the congress was addressed to all disciplines that deal with the Greco-Roman civilization and their neighbouring cultures from the Aegean Bronze Age to the end of Late Antiquity.

The participation of more than 1.200 scholars from more than 40 countries demonstrates the great response to the topic of the congress. Altogether, more than 900 papers in 128 panels were presented, as were more than 110 posters. The publication of the congress is in two stages: larger panels are initially presented as independent volumes, such as this publication. Finally, at the end of the editing process, all contributions will be published in a joint conference volume.

We would like to take this opportunity to thank all participants and helpers of the congress who made it such a great success. Its realization would not have been possible without the generous support of many institutions, whom we would like to thank once again: the Universities of Bonn and Cologne, the Archaeological Society of Cologne, the Archaeology Foundation of Cologne, the Gerda Henkel Foundation, the Fritz Thyssen Foundation, the Sal. Oppenheim Foundation, the German Research Foundation (DFG), the German Academic Exchange Service (DAAD), the Romano-Germanic Museum Cologne and the LVR-LandesMuseum Bonn. Finally, our thanks go to all colleagues and panel organizers who were involved in the editing and printing process.

Bonn/Cologne, in August 2019

Martin Bentz & Michael Heinzelmann

The Rural Foundations of The Roman Economy. New Approaches to Rome's Ancient Countryside from the Archaic to the Early Imperial Period: Introduction

Peter Attema – Günther Schörner

Since the 1960s, excavations, survey and environmental studies have generated a wealth of data on the countryside around Rome north and south of the Tiber. Data pertain to rural settlement types ranging from the small farmstead to the large villa, and regard non-urban burial grounds, production facilities, such as pottery kilns, smithies and quarries, as well as infrastructure and field systems. Also, a growing interest can be noted in such important issues as crop choice, manuring, land reclamation and land degradation. In combination, this wealth of information, often still unconnected, can inform us on the functioning and performance of the Roman economy in a crucial period of Rome's rise to power during the Archaic and mid-Republican periods. It can also be used to investigate its subsequent development during the Late Republican and Early Imperial period within the expanding Mediterranean economic network of that period.

The aim of the session "The Rural Foundations of The Roman Economy. New Approaches to Rome's Ancient Countryside from the Archaic to the Early Imperial Period" was to bring together methodologically informed, data-driven studies that shed light on the drivers and performance of the Central Italian rural economy during the Archaic to Imperial period.[1] The session was accepted as part of the theme "Methodology: Survey archaeology, natural sciences, quantification", one of the overarching themes defined by the organizers of the 19th International Congress of Classical Archaeology on Archaeology and Economy in the Ancient World. The original session was split up chronologically with a set of papers reflecting on the Archaic and Mid-Republican period first and then followed by a set of papers focusing on the Late Republican and Imperial periods. However, for the publication we have chosen to start with papers offering a broad synthetic perspective and to zoom in afterwards on case studies of regional and local relevance.

The first paper by José Ernesto Moura Knust (Instituto Federal Fluminense, Rio de Janeiro) entitled "Far from the Walls. Explaining Rural Settlement Dispersal within Roman, Mediterranean and Global Frameworks" advocates to view Roman rural settlement not as a unique phenomenon but rather as part of a Mediterranean-wide historical process that requires a Mediterranean or even global historical framework for explanation. According to Knust, factors that should be taken into account are climate, connectivity leading to exchange of agricultural technology (including tools and crops), commercialization, and demographic pressure. In such an explanatory framework he sees agricultural intensification as the main driver leading to dispersed rural settlement in the ancient world, although in world history nucleated scenarios (as in the medieval period) occur as well.

The second methodological paper by Stephen Collins-Elliot (University of Tennessee) focuses on the application of computational methods to data mined from *Forma Italiae* publications. His focus is on the economy of the Suburbium of Rome; he aims to study this topic not only in terms of the increase or decrease of (classes of) rural sites but also in terms of production, trade and consumption, using amphorae and items pertaining to craft production (textiles, glass, ceramics, iron). His pilot study shows the potential of aggregating data for categorical data analysis even if data were produced with different field and artefact collection methods.

The third contribution by Peter Attema, Tymon de Haas, Gijs Tol and Jorn Seubers raises the potential of integrated datasets from archaeological survey for economic and demographic analyses of the Roman rural landscape. The paper presents the database that has been created for the Pontine Region, south of Rome, holding data of over 30 years of field survey. The paper reviews analyses that were done with this data. In addition, the paper presents the current initiative by a consortium of universities to make their respective databases part of one overarching structure – The Roman Hinterland database – geared at socio-economic and demographic analyses of the Suburbium of Rome writ large. The databases that are currently being merged concern the Suburbium project database created by Sapienza University, the Tiber Valley Project database of the British School at Rome (with partners based at the universities of St. Andrews and Durham), and the Pontine Region Project database created at the Groningen Archaeological Institute (with affiliated researchers at the universities of Melbourne and Leiden). Attention is drawn to such fundamental issues as site classification and dating.

The fourth contribution is by Alessandro Launaro, and is submitted as an extended abstract with reference to with reference to a paper recently published in the Journal of Roman Archaeology (Launaro, A., & Leone, N. (2018). A view from the margin? Roman commonwares and patterns of distribution and consumption at Interamna Lirenas (Lazio). Journal of Roman Archaeology, 31, 323–338. doi:10.1017/S1047759418001356 (with N. Leone). In it, the author updates us on the results of the Interamna Lirenas survey in the Liri valley in South Lazio, a Roman town and its hinterland located in the border zone between old Latium and Campania. Launaro poses the problem of reduced archaeological visibility of archeological landscapes due to limited presence of imported pottery in the early Imperial Period, as is the case with Interamna in both town and countryside, and how the study of common wares may substitute a picture of economic decline with one of stable regional relevance instead.

The fifth contribution, by Veronika Schreck and Günther Schörner of the University of Vienna, investigates the economic relationship between the Roman town of Empoli and the rural site of Molino San Vincenzo in the valley landscape of the rivers Pesa and Orme in present-day Tuscany. The focus of the paper is on the analysis of an urban archaeological context from Empoli that yielded a huge amount of unstratified pottery. A sophisticated analysis of the pottery assemblage proved instructive for understanding the different ratios between local production and imports in comparison with the pottery from Molino San Vicenzo, a location more remote from the main infrastructure.

With respect to the topic of archaeological visibility of rural landscapes and the agrarian practices taking place in them, the sixth paper by Anna Maria Mercuri et al. shows the important contribution archaeobotanical studies can make to understanding local rural economies. The study of pollen, plant macroremains, charcoal, fungi and other faunal remains may reveal aspects of the farmed landscape at different scales as well as the environmental conditions in which farming took place. Such information may range from the actual crops cultivated in the fields to their on-site processing. The Roman Peasant Project, directed by Kimberly Bowles, forms the framework for the following paper. The close collaboration between the palaeobotanists of the University of Modena and Reggio Emila and the international group of archaeologists working in the project proved fundamental to understanding the function of a range of small rural find spots found in the archaeological survey, some of which were excavated.

Two papers presented in the session have not evolved in contributions. One was by Gabriele Cifani of the Università degli studi di Roma "Tor Vergata" on the rural economy of early Rome. In his paper, Cifani discussed the excavations of a number of rural buildings recently investigated in the suburb of Rome as historical documents to reconstruct the economy of Rome and central Tyrrhenian Italy in the Archaic period. During the sixth century BC there was a significant population increase in Etruria and Latium, as revealed by the rise in the number of archaeological sites and the beginning of the systematic production of wine and olive oil. Survey data testify to this new territorial organization; for the first time, scattered open sites appear at some scale. Archaeological evidence further suggests an agricultural strategy beyond one of mere subsistence, and is comparable to the ones recorded in the contemporary rural landscapes of Etruria and Greece. Olive and wine cultivation imply the evolution of land property rights, a greater sophistication of the agricultural sector in terms of culture and organization, the need for a more specialized labor force, and the growth of an entangled economy. Simon Stoddart (University of Cambridge) talked (also on behalf of Letizia Ceccarelli), about the incorporation of rural settlement into the Roman world and production on the frontier between Etruria and Umbria. Recent work, in collaboration with Marco Amadei, Jeremy Bennett and Nicholas Whitehead, concerned the potential frontier between Etruscan Perugia and Umbrian Gubbio, which lies close to the watershed north of Montelabate (Perugia). Systematic field survey on the Gaslini estate has established an interesting local trajectory for the incorporation of a probable Etruscan enclave on the left bank of the Tiber into the Roman world. Within the immediate area of Montelabate only three sites, Civitella Benazzone, Civitella d'Arna and Col di Marzo appear to have been occupied in the Etruscan period. Excavations at the small and naturally defended center of Col di Marzo suggest an occupation from the fifth century BC until the first half of the third century BC. Incorporation within the Roman political orbit first led to a complete abandonment of the area. Gradually from the late first century BC onwards, small farmsteads began to be inserted, reaching a peak in the early Imperial period. The excavation of a kiln complex close to Montelabate itself suggests the economic motive for this demographic shift that occurred in two distinct phases from the first until the fifth century AD. In the first phase, the local landscape was part of a network of wine supply for the major population of Rome and the local market for over two hundred years. This led to the production of flatter bottomed amphorae suitable for shallow draft river craft which could have navigated the Tiber from a point just below the site. The gentle slopes of the low hills of the Apennines were highly suitable for wine and olive production, whilst also offering clays of reasonable quality, limestone for temper, and plentiful wood supplies for firing the kilns. In a second stage, the kilns were employed for the production of tiles and coarse wares, serving a local economy. From the study of this small region this paper provided insight into the microeconomics of the Roman empire.

The session as a whole was successful as it succeeded to relate different scales of inquiry into the Roman economy over a long period from the Archaic period well into the Imperial period with a sharp focus on the suburbium of Rome *sensu lato.* It showed how important it is that we test existing historical and archaeological models on the rural economy of Rome and its hinterland with (aggregated) data derived from landscape archaeology. At the same time, these also need to be corrected by empirical research on micro-regional landscape archaeological research and excavation on individual rural sites. In the developing era of 'big data' we need to keep a neat balance between quantitative abstraction and qualitative observation.

Wim Jongman, in his concluding paper 'The voice of the silent majority: Archaeological surveys and the history of the Roman countryside', reflects on the papers presented at the conference and published in this volume. He emphasizes the important role that archaeological data from archeological landscape survey and excavations of rural sites play in the current debate on the nature of the Roman agricultural economy, and how this debate should connect with the comparative historical debates of preindustrial economies and societies.

Notes

[1] Panel 11.1: The Rural Foundations of The Roman Economy. New Approaches to Rome's Ancient Countryside from the Archaic to the Early Imperial Period was organized by Peter Attema (University of Groningen), Gabriele Cifani (Tor Vergata, Rome), Günther Schörner (University of Vienna) and was held on Wednesday, 23 May 2018, 09:00–13:30.

Far from the Walls. Explaining Rural Settlement Dispersal within Roman, Mediterranean and Global Frameworks

José Ernesto Moura Knust

Abstract

One of the most outstanding findings of field surveys in South Etruria and Lazio was the identification of an expansive pattern of rural settlement dispersion along the Roman conquest of these regions (fifth to third century BC). Since the sixties, these findings have reshaped our images of the Roman countryside. Although the Roman pacification of the region initially was advanced as the crucial factor, soon the discovery of coeval similar patterns in regions of the Mediterranean outside of the area of Roman conquest urged other ways of explaining it. The purpose of this paper is to survey and evaluate the ways in which different scholars have tried to explain the dispersion of rural settlement on a Mediterranean scale. I analyse and compare the theoretical and methodological bases of these explanations to identify the general outlines of the current state of the debate. Then, I will consider this current state of the debate in a broader framework. I intend to reframe the dispersion of the Mediterranean settlement within a larger narrative of the global history of the development of complex agrarian societies, and of the specific way in which the Mediterranean countryside developed one.

Introduction

Since the post-war period, Tyrrhenian central Italy has been surveyed by several archaeological projects.[1] One of their most outstanding results is the identification of an expansive pattern of rural settlement dispersion during the Roman conquest of these regions. Since the seminal South Etruria Survey, a large number of small sites, identified by the dispersion of scattered material datable to the "Roman period", has been one of the most ubiquitous findings of surveys in Tyrrhenian central Italy.[2] There are plenty of methodological issues concerning these findings, ranging from technical questions of material visibility on the ground to conceptual questions of how to interpret and classify these sites.[3] I am not going to address these here, so I will develop my ideas from a simple assumption about them: the increasing number of small isolated sites in rural contexts in Tyrrhenian central Italy during the third quarter of the first millennium BC is a real (although not exactly proportional) index of increasing human occupation of the countryside.

Accepting this assumption provides a picture of expanding occupation of the countryside of Tyrrhenian central Italy in an increasing number of key areas by small and discrete structures in these centuries. "Settlement dispersal" is a common label used to describe the process, since these field surveys identified the abandonment of many fortified hilltop settlements during this period that had dominated in previous centuries.[4] Anyway, it is important to consider two points: first, this was a time of increasing urbanization in this region;[5] and second, recent work on minor centres, such as *fora* and road stations, reveal that a complex hierarchical settlement pattern was emerging.[6] Therefore, this dispersal of rural settlement was part of the development of a broader and more complex human occupation, with a more marked distinction between urban and rural settlements.

The aim of this paper is to sketch a general framework to make sense of how the change of settlement patterns that occurred in Tyrrhenian central Italy – *and beyond* – in the third quarter of the first millennium BC has been explained. Some decades ago, the first attempts to explain this process only considered the areas under Roman power. Later, scholars expanded their perspectives, using a new "Mediterranean framework" instead of the previous "Roman framework". In my final remarks I will provide some thoughts on how to develop these ideas into an even broader perspective, in the direction of the trend for a global history.

From the Roman to the Mediterranean Framework

The first attempts to explain this settlement change came from the archaeologists involved in the South Etruria Survey. Their hypotheses differ slightly between them but have a common core. On the one hand is the idea that Roman conquest brought peace and political stability to the region, allowing local peasants to live far from the walls. G. D. B. Jones, taking the *ager Capenas* into account, for instance, took this direction.[7] On the other hand is the idea that Roman power promoted this settlement dispersal either because of military or economic concerns. As Tim Potter stated, Romans desired the removal of people from easily defensible sites to avoid resistance as well as the occupation of new lands to raise levels of agricultural production.[8] In the end, both hypotheses take the Roman conquest as the historical context and the Roman State as the historical agent of the settlement change.

These two elements of this Roman framework have been criticized. Taking the Roman State as the main subject of settlement history is certainly anachronistic, because it assumes the early Roman state was a modern nation-state able to develop coherent and broad policies in its territory. Nonetheless, political history and state theory have been stressing the importance of analysing pre-modern states with specific approaches and categories.[9] Especially important to my argument, scholars studying early Roman colonization have shown that this historical process cannot be understood as an exclusively Roman process or solely as a state initiative.[10]

It is also important to bear in mind the fact that many wars took place in Italy after its conquest by Rome – at least until the Civil Wars in the waning years of the Republic. Besides this, the end of wars did not mean complete pacification of the countryside.[11] Hence, isolated settlements inside Roman territory were not totally secure, and a more peaceful countryside seems not to be a sufficient cause for settlement dispersal.

The most persuasive criticism of the Roman Framework, however, is empirical. Nicola Terrenato has pointed that if we avoid a kind of Roman myopia, coeval processes of settlement dispersal can be identified in areas outside of those controlled by Rome.[12] In central Italy, surveys have identified settlements dispersed before the Roman conquest – for example, in the Rieti Basin.[13] In southern Italy many surveys have identified similar processes, like in the hinterlands of Sybaris and Metaponto, and in different areas of the Salento isthmus as well.[14] But this is not solely a peninsular trend. In different areas of the central Mediterranean basin, like Sicily, Sardinia and North Africa, surveys have also identified similar processes.[15] The same trend can be found in areas of the western[16] and eastern Mediterranean.[17] This is not a Mediterranean process in the sense that every region of the Mediterranean basin experienced it. But it is a Mediterranean trend in the sense that different areas around this region of the globe experienced it.

Here I must note that there are complicated methodological issues concerning the comparison of different surveys.[18] I will, however, not address these here, and work with the assumption that despite the different meaning given by each survey to the identification of dispersed archaeological material datable to the period of concern, they can be interpreted in a general sense of increasing scope and complexity of human occupation. This is the core historical process that we are facing in the Mediterranean basin, beginning in the second quarter of the first millennium BC and gaining significant momentum in the third quarter of that millennium: the development of social, economic and political complexity.[19] This settlement change is one of its faces.

A Mediterranean historical process requires a Mediterranean Framework for explanation. And scholars have been exploring it in recent decades. What most evidently links the settlement histories of these different Mediterranean regions is the Mediterranean itself. First, it has a climatic feature: the unifying Mediterranean climate of the region. For example, Willem Jongman pointed to climatic change as an important factor in the growth of the Mediterranean economy during the second half of the first millennium BC.[20] Better climatic conditions that increased agricultural productivity, for instance, would have resulted in increased population and therefore occupation of new lands and/or the intensification of agriculture, both related to settlement expansion and increasing complexity. More specific studies of the paleoclimatology of the Mediterranean basin are still incipient, so little information is available on how general climate changes affected specific areas. Therefore, we must be careful with climatic hypotheses.[21]

The second way in which the Mediterranean Sea could link these settlement histories is by its connectivity.[22] This has both demographic and economic features, since people as well as goods flowed through these connections. Local or regional demographic growths could affect the entire Mediterranean by migration and colonization processes. The well-known Greek and Roman colonizations are part of a broader history of population movement through the Mediterranean. In this sense, a possible demographic increase would have caused settlement dispersal in different parts of the Mediterranean area. In fact, some scholars, like de Haas and Yntema, pointed to demographic pressure as the main cause of settlement dispersal in the areas they studied.[23]

Besides demographic pressure, the diffusion of specific kinds of crops, farming techniques and instruments through the Mediterranean basin could have led to the intensification of agriculture and higher per capita productivity. There is a longstanding debate on the agrarian systems of the ancient Mediterranean,[24] but its most recent developments point to the existence of a variety of agrarian systems coexisting in the area.[25] So, it is important to notice the historical development and diffusion of more intensive agrarian systems in different regions of the Mediterranean basin to understand its economic foundations. We have good data to understand the diffusion of labour-intensive crops like grapes and olives during the second and third quarters of the first millennium BC.[26] Moreover, we have evidence of the diffusion of iron farming tools around the Mediterranean, especially important to the expansion of agriculture in heavier soils.[27] There is some evidence of increased animal husbandry and the use of manure, as well as the development and diffusion of irrigation and drainage techniques.[28] In the big picture, we have a solid image of intensification and expansion of Mediterranean agriculture during these centuries.

The increasing commercialization of production is usually suggested as the main cause of agricultural intensification, and thus of settlement change. Studying the South Argolid, Curtis Runnels and Tjeerd Van Andel stated that "the number and density of settlements increased, usually with an increase of population, whenever access to external commercial markets was available".[29] In this model, the possibility of earning profits stimulated the intensification of production, which demanded more dispersed settlement. Therefore, the development of maritime trade can explain settlement dispersal along the Mediterranean coast, and there is also solid evidence of more comprehensive Mediterranean economic integration.

In this sense, we must explain further why this integration took place. Runnels and Van Andel take market relations as a natural development of historical economies; as soon as it was possible for Mediterranean people to connect in market relationships, they did so. But there are two alternative ways to explain the increase of trade and economic integration in the Mediterranean basin. On the one hand, Horden and Purcell identify the circulation of goods as part of the Mediterranean peasantry's strategy to avoid insecurity.[30] On the other hand, Peter Bang states that the "substance of pre-capitalist commerce is the product of surplus extraction – rather than the product of labor division seeking profits".[31] Taking these approaches, then, the explanation for this process can be linked to the strategies of an increasing peasant population to avoid risk as well as of the ruling classes to increase surplus extraction. Regarding Mediterranean ruling classes, it is important to bear in mind that the development of Roman power in central Italy was part of a broader Mediterranean context of expanding imperial powers. These included the Hellenistic kingdoms in the eastern Mediterranean, some powerful Greek cities in southern Italy, and the Carthaginians in North Africa and the western Mediterranean.

From the Mediterranean to a Global Framework

To sum up, the explanation for the change of settlement patterns inside the Mediterranean framework can be sketched along the following lines. The dispersion of rural settlement in different places in the Mediterranean basin was related to: 1) some possible climatic changes that improved conditions for Mediterranean agriculture (which allowed intensification and expansion of cultivated areas); 2) the probable development of new farming implements and techniques, as well the diffusion of some crops (which also allowed intensification and expansion of cultivated areas); 3) the clear intensification of the circulation of products and integration of the Mediterranean basin (which encouraged intensification and expansion of cultivated areas); 4) and *last but not least,* the visible formation of dominant supralocal and imperial classes in several of these regions (which pushed intensification and expansion of cultivated areas).

As can be noted, intensification of agriculture is at the heart of the framework to explain this change in settlement patterns. And here lies a problem. The more perennial presence of farmers suggested by the existence of such structures is coherent with intensification of agriculture. However, this is not a necessary relationship. There are famous cases of agrarian intensification coeval with nucleation of rural settlement, the most evident case being Medieval Europe, when what some call the "medieval agrarian revolution" is correlated with the emergence of peasant villages.[32]

We need to use the *jeux d'échelles.* The Mediterranean framework has been important to identify new questions and models of analysis. However, there are different processes that demand more specific or broader scales of analysis. First, let me take some examples of more specific scales of analysis that can be useful to understand the change in settlement pattern. Even if the idea of pacification is flawed, changes in warfare, such as lesser risk of raids, can be an important local or regional factor to understand the settlement history. Worker exploitation might have played an important role as well, as suggested by Stephen Hodkinson, who related the settlement pattern in Laconia and Messenia with Spartan helotism.[33] Moreover, Carter,[34] studying Metaponto, and Terrenato,[35] writing about early Roman times, related changes in settlement patterns with changes in land ownership schemes. It is important, therefore, to combine these different scales of analyses to produce convincing historical explanations.

In the opposite direction, there is room to consider whether the Mediterranean scale is the broadest scale that can be studied regarding the settlement process. Some scholars have been stressing the need to go further and place the Mediterranean in the context of global history.[36] The Mediterranean scale is between the scale of specific societies (or "civilizations") and the broader scale of global comparisons or global history. So, if it allows us to go beyond some limits of the former, the combination of both with the global scale can be important as well.

The ancient Mediterranean has indeed been placed inside global comparativism in recent decades. Comparisons between the ancient Mediterranean and East Asia, especially between the Roman and Chinese empires, and broader comparison between ancient empires including the Roman Empire, were made by important scholars like Walter Scheidel and Peter Bang.[37] However, what I want to propose here is slightly different. Some global historians have proposed what they call relational and historical global comparativism. It consists of the study of historical connections and entanglements between different societies that drive their coeval historical processes, comparing those different but connected histories. This allows us to go beyond the more usual formal study of structural similarities and differences between discrete societies. Along these lines we must go beyond comparing the Mediterranean with other areas of the globe and place the Mediterranean *into* the global connections.

But which connections? Talking about a different topic, the Italian scholar Aldo Schiavone, in his book *The End of the Past,* suggested a thoughtful idea of a specific Mediterranean path in a broader historical development led by the Neolithic Revolution.[38] The picture that Schiavone paints is a primeval process rooted in the transition to agrarian and state societies in the Near East expanding to different regions and taking different paths. We can root the historical developments of the Iron Age Mediterranean in a deeper history of Western Eurasia using this image. It can be useful in two different temporalities and two different approaches to better understand the increasing complexity around the Mediterranean in the Iron Age, of which the change in settlement pattern is part.

Talking about the approaches, we can work with the identification of connections and entanglements among these different global regions and the consequences as well as comparisons among the different paths by which these regions developed. This can be done in two temporalities. The first is a very *longue durée,* or deep history, which identifies the deep layers of historical sedimentation deposited by those connections on which the historical processes happens. The second analyses the synchronic temporality of coeval and connected historical processes. This global history approach sounds very fruitful to the study of the process described in this paper. Some of the processes envisioned in the Mediterranean framework are easily recognizable as broader processes. The diffusion of ironworking is the most obvious example. If we zoom out spatially and chronologically, we can grasp the diffusion of agrarian systems and crops around the Mediterranean on the same scale, since Mediterranean farming systems are historical products of the Near Eastern centre of agriculture origin.

Notes

[1] Syntheses in Goodchild 2013; Terrenato 2012.

[2] Duncan – Reynolds 1958; Hemphill, 1975; Jones, 1962, 1963; Kahane et al. 1968; Potter, 1979.

[3] Barker 1991; Schörner 2012; Terrenato 2000; Witcher 2006, 2012.

[4] Goodchild 2013, 200; Terrenato 2012, 147–149.

[5] Andersen 1997; Attema 2004; Osborne – Cunliffe, 2005.

[6] Tol et al. 2014.

[7] Jones 1963, 129.

[8] Potter 1979, 93.

[9] Hespanha 2012; Spruyt 1994.

[10] Bispham 2006; Bradley 2006; Pelgrom 2012; Pelgrom – Stek 2014.

[11] E.g. Varro *De Re Rustica* 1.12.4 on the danger of bandits' raids.

[12] Terrenato 2012, 147

[13] Coccia et al. 1992, 1995.

[14] Attema et al. 2010; Carter 2006; Yntema 1993.

[15] Fentress – Docter, 2008; van Dommelen – Finocchi, 2008; van Dommelen et al. 2008.

[16] Gómez Bellard 2008; López Castro 2008.

[17] Alcock 1994.

[18] Alcock – Cherry, 2004.

[19] Attema et al. 2010.

[20] Jongman 2014.

[21] Luterbacher et al. 2012; Manning 2013, 106. 108.

[22] Horden – Purcell 2000.

[23] De Haas 2011, 93; Yntema 1993, 186.

[24] Traditional approach in Jardé, 1925; Michell 1940; Semple 1932. Critics in Halstead 1987. Debate on Attica: Gallant 1982; Garnsey 1989, 93 f.; Jameson 1978 *versus* Isager – Skydsgaard 2001, 108–113; Sallares 1991, 300 f.

[25] On intensive farming in Roman times: Kron, 2000, 2005.

[26] Brun 2004, 80–88; Sallares 1991, 305 f.

[27] Attema et al. 2010, 90; Craddock, 1995, 259 f.; van Joolen 2003, 113; van Dommelen – Gómez Bellard 2008, 236.

[28] On the debate of off-site material as evidence for manuring: Alcock et al. 1994; Bintliff – Snodgrass 1988, 508; Coccia et al. 1995; De Haas 2012, 60 f.; Fentress 2000; Hayes 1991. On literary evidence for manuring: Kron 2008, 76; Pliny Naturalia Historia, 17.50; Columella De Re Rustica, 2.15.1; Palladius Opus Agriculturae, 10.3.2. On *cuniculi:* Attema 1993, 223 f.; Judson – Kahane 1963, 88 f.; Ravelli – Howart 1984.

[29] Runnels – Andel 1987, 303.

[30] Horden – Purcell 2000.

[31] Bang 2008.

[32] On the medieval agrarian revolution: Duby 1968; Dyer 1989; Fossier 2015; Lopez 1976. On the *encellulement:* Curtis 2013; Fossier 1982.

[33] Hodkinson 2008.

[34] Carter 1990.

[35] Terrenato 2012, 148.

[36] Harris 2005; Horden – Purcell 2006.

[37] Bang – Kolodziejczyk 2012; Scheidel 2015.

[38] Schiavone 2002.

References

Alcock 1994

S. E. Alcock. Breaking up the Hellenistic World: Survey and Society, in: I. Morris (ed.), Classical Greece: Ancient Histories and Modern Archaeologies (Cambridge 1994).

Alcock – Cherry 2004

S. E. Alcock – J. F. Cherry (eds.), Side-by-side Survey: Comparative Regional Studies in the Mediterranean World (Oxford 2004).

Alcock et al. 1994

S. E. Alcock – J. F. Cherry – J. L. Davis, Intensive Survey, Agricultural Practice and the Classical Landscape of Greece, in: I. Morris (ed.), Classical Greece: Ancient Histories and Modern Archaeologies (Cambridge 1994).

Damgaard Andersen 1997

H. Damgaard Andersen. Urbanization in the Mediterranean in the 9th to 6th Centuries BC (Copenhagen 1997).

Attema 1993

P. A. J. Attema. An Archaeological Survey in the Pontine Region. A Contribution to the Early Settlement History of South Lazio, 900–100 BC (Vols. 1–2) (Groningen 1993).

Attema 2004

P. A. J. Attema (ed.), Centralization, Early Urbanization, and Colonization in first Millenium B.C. Italy and Greece (Leuven 2004).

Attema et al. 2010

P. A. J. Attema – G.-J. L. M. Burgers – M. van Leusen, Regional Pathways to Complexity: Settlement and Land-use Dynamics in Early Italy from the Bronze Age to the Republican Period (Amsterdam 2010).

Bang 2008

P. Bang. The Roman Bazaar: a Comparative Study of Trade and Markets in a Tributary Empire (Cambridge 2008).

Bang – Kolodziejczyk 2012

P. Bang – D. Kolodziejczyk, Universal Empire: A Comparative Approach to Imperial Culture and Representation in Eurasian History (Cambridge 2012).

Barker 1991

G. Barker, Approaches to Archaeological Survey, in: G. Barker – J. Lloyd (eds.), Roman Landscapes: Archaeological Survey in the Mediterranean Region (London 1991).

Bintliff – Snodgrass 1988

J. Bintliff – A. Snodgrass, Off-Site Pottery Distributions: A Regional and Interregional Perspective, Current Anthropology 29, 1988, 506–513.

Bispham 2006

E. Bispham, Coloniam deducere: How Roman was Roman Colonization during the Middle Republic, in: J.-P. Wilson – E. Bispham – G. J. Bradley (eds.), Greek and Roman Colonization: Origins, Ideologies and Interactions (Swansea 2006).

Bradley 2006

G. J. Bradley. Colonization and Identity in Republican Italy, in: J.-P. Wilson – E. Bispham – G. J. Bradley (eds.), Greek and Roman Colonization: Origins, Ideologies and Interactions (Swansea 2006).

Brun 2004

J.-P. Brun. Archéologie du vin et de l'huile de la préhistoire à l'époque hellénistique. (Paris 2004).

Carter 1990

J. C. Carter, Metapontum: Land, Wealth and Population, in: J. P. Descoeudres (ed.), Greek Colonists and Native Populations: Proceedings of the first Australian Congress of Classical Archaeology (Oxford 1990).

Carter 2006

J. C. Carter, Discovering the Greek Countryside at Metaponto (Ann Arbor 2006).

Coccia et al. 1992

S. Coccia – D. Mattingly – P. Beavitt – H. Elton – P. Foss – I. George – K. Morton, Settlement History, Environment and Human Exploitation of an Intermontane Basin in the Central Apennines: The Rieti Survey 1988–1991 Part I, BSR 60, 1992, 213–289.

Coccia et al. 1995

S. Coccia – D. Mattingly – P. Beavitt – H. Elton – P. Foss – I. George – T. Sudell, Settlement History, Environment and Human Exploitation of an Intermontane Basin in the Central Apennines: The Rieti Survey 1988–1991 Part II. Land-Use Patterns and Gazetteer, BSR 63, 1995, 105–158.

Craddock 1995

P. Craddock, Early Metal Mining and Production (Edinburgh 1995).

Curtis 2013

D. Curtis, The Emergence of Concentrated Villages in Medieval Western Europe: Explanatory Frameworks in the Historiography, Canadian Journal of History 48, 2013, 223–251.

De Haas 2011

T. De Haas, Fields, Farms and Colonists: Intensive Field Survey and Early Roman Colonization in the Pontine Region, Central Italy (Eelde 2011).

De Haas 2012
T. De Haas, Beyond Dots on the Map: Intensive Survey Data and the Interpretation of Small Sites and Off-site Interpretation, in: P. Attema – G. Schörner (eds.), Comparative Issues in the Archaeology of the Roman Rural Landscape: Site Classification between Survey, Excavation and Historical Categories (Portsmouth 2012).

Duby 1968
G. Duby, Rural Economy and Country Life in the Medieval West (London 1968).

Duncan – Reynolds 1958
G. Duncan – J. M. Reynolds, Sutri (Sutrium): Notes on Southern Etruria 3, BSR 26, 1958, 63–134.

Dyer 1989
C. Dyer, Standards of Living in the Later Middle Ages: Social Change in England C.1200–1520 (Cambridge 1989).

Fentress 2000
E. Fentress, What Are We Counting For?, in: R. Francovich – H. Patterson (eds.), Extracting Meaning from Ploughsoil Assemblages (Oxford 2000).

Fentress – Docter 2008
E. Fentress – R. F. Docter, North Africa: Rural Settelement and Agricultural Production, in: P. A. R. van Dommelen – C. Gómez Bellard (eds.), Rural Landscapes of the Punic World (London 2008).

Fossier 1982
R. Fossier. Enfance de l'Europe: Xe–XIIe siècles: aspects économiques et sociaux. (Paris 1982).

Fossier 2015
R. Fossier, Rural Economy and Demographic Growth, in: D. Luscombe – J. Riley-Smith (eds.), The New Cambridge Medieval History 4, c.1024–c.1198 (Cambridge 2015).

Gallant 1982
T. W. Gallant, Agricultural Systems, Land Tenure, and the Reforms of Solon, BSA 77, 1982, 111–124.

Garnsey 1989
P. Garnsey, Famine and Food Supply in the Graeco-Roman World: Responses to Risk and Crisis (Cambridge 1989).

Gómez Bellard 2008
C. Gómez Bellard, Ibiza: the Making of New Landscape, in: P. van Dommelen – C. Gómez Bellard (eds.), Rural landscapes of the Punic World (London 2008).

Goodchild 2013
H. Goodchild, Agriculture and the Environment of Republican Italy, in: J. D. Evans (ed.), A Companion to the Archaeology of the Roman Republic (Chichester 2013).

Halstead 1987
P. Halstead, Traditional and Ancient Rural Economy in Mediterranean Europe: plus ça change?, JHS 107, 1987, 77–87.

Harris 2005
W. V. Harris, The Mediterranean and Ancient History, in: W. V. Harris (ed.), Rethinking the Mediterranean (Oxford 2005).

Hayes 1991
P. P. Hayes, Models for the Distribution of Pottery around former Agricultural Settlements, in: A. J. Schofield, Interpreting Artefact Scatters: Contributions to Ploughzone Archaeology (Oxford 1991).
Hemphill 1975
P. Hemphill, The Cassia-Clodia Survey, BSR 43, 1975, 118–172.
Hespanha 2012
A. M. Hespanha, Caleidoscópio do antigo regime (São Paulo 2012).
Hodkinson 2008
S. Hodkinson, Spartiates, Helots and the Direction of the Agrarian Economy: toward an Understanding of Helotage in Comparative Perspective, in: C. Katsari – E. Dal Lago (eds.), Slave Systems: Ancient and Modern (Cambridge 2008).
Horden – Purcell 2000
P. Horden – N. Purcell, The Corrupting Sea: A Study of Mediterranean History (Oxford 2000).
Horden – Purcell 2006
P. Horden – N. Purcell, The Mediterranean and the New Thalassology. The American Historical Review 111, 2006, 722–740.
Isager – Skydsgaard 2001
S. Isager – J. E. Skydsgaard, Ancient Greek Agriculture: An Introduction (London 2001).
Jameson 1978
M. H. Jameson, Agriculture and Slavery in Classical Athens, ClJ 73, 1978, 122–145.
Jardé 1925
A. Jardé. Les Céréales dans l'antiquité grecque (Paris 1925).
Jones 1962
G. D. B. Jones. Capena and the Ager Capenas, BSR 30, 1962, 116–207.
Jones 1963
G. D. B. Jones, Capena and the Ager Capenas: Part II, BSR 31, 1963, 100–158.
Jongman 2014
W. Jongman, Re-constucting the Roman Economy, in: L. Neal – J. G. Williamson (eds.), The Cambridge History of Capitalism (Cambridge 2014).
van Joolen 2003
E. van Joolen, Archaeological Land Evaluation: A Reconstruction of the Suitability of Ancient Landscapes for Various Land Uses in Italy Focused on the First Millennium BC (Groningen 2003).
Judson – Kahane 1963
S. Judson – A. Kahane, Underground Drainageways in Southern Etruria and Northern Latium, BSR 31, 1963, 74–99.
Kahane et al. 1968
A. Kahane – L. M. Threipland – J. B. Ward-Perkins, The 'Ager Veientanus', North and East of Rome, BSR 36, 1968.
Kron 2000
G. Kron, Roman ley-farming, JRA 13, 2000, 227–287.

Kron 2005

G. Kron, Sustainble Roman Intensive Mixed Farming Methods: Water Conservation and Erosion Control, in: R. Bedon – E. Hermon (eds.), Concepts, pratiques et enjeux environnementaux dans l'empire romain (Limoges 2005).

Kron 2008

G. Kron, The Much Maligned Peasant. Comparative Perspectives on the Productivity of the Small Farmer in Classical Antiquity, in: L. de Ligt – S. Northwood, People, Land, and Politics: Demographic Developments and the Transformation of Roman Italy 300 BC–AD 14 (Leiden 2008).

López Castro 2008

J. L. López Castro, The Iberian Peninsula: Landscapes of Tradition, in: P. van Dommelen – C. Gómez Bellard (eds.), Rural Landscapes of the Punic World (London 2008).

Lopez 1976

R. S. Lopez, The Commercial Revolution of the Middle Ages, 950–1350 (Cambridge 1976).

Luterbacher et al. 2012.

J. Luterbacher – R. García-Herrera – S. Akcer-Ori – M.-C. Alvarez-Castro – G. Benito – J. Booth – U. Büntgen, A Review of 2000 Years of Paleoclimatic Evidence in the Mediterranean, in: P. Lionello (ed.), The Climate of the Mediterranean Region: From the Past to the Future (London 2012).

Manning 2013

S. W. Manning, The Roman World and Climate: Context, Relevance of Climate Change, and Some Issues, in: W. V. Harris (ed.), The Ancient Mediterranean Environment between Science and History (Leiden 2013).

Michell 1940

H. Michell, The Economics of Ancient Greece (Cambridge 1940).

Osborne – Cunliffe 2005

R. Osborne – B. Cunliffe, Mediterranean Urbanization 800–600 BC (Oxford 2005).

Pelgrom 2012

J. Pelgrom, Demography, Settlement Organization and Impact of Colonies founded by Rome (Leiden 2012).

Pelgrom – Stek 2014

J. Pelgrom – T. D. Stek, Roman Colonization under the Republic: Historiographical Contextualization of a Paradigm, in: J. Pelgrom – T. D. Stek (eds.), Roman Republican Colonisation: new Perspectives from Archaeology and Ancient History (Portsmouth 2014).

Potter 1979

T. W. Potter, The Changing Landscape of South Etruria (London 1979).

Ravelli – Howart 1984

F. Ravelli – P. Howart. Etruscan cuniculi: Tunnels for the Collection of Pure Water. In Transactions of the Twelfth International Congress on Irrigation and Drainage 2 (Fort Collins 1984).

Runnels – van Andel 1987

C. N. Runnels – T. H. Andel, The Evolution of Settlement in the Southern Argolid, Greece: An Economic Explanation, Hesperia 56, 1987, 303–334.

Sallares 1991

R. Sallares, The Ecology of the Ancient Greek World (London 1991).

Scheidel 2015

W. Scheidel (ed.), State Power in Ancient China and Rome (Oxford 2015).

Schiavone 2002

A. Schiavone, The End of the Past: Ancient Rome and the Modern West (Cambridge 2002).

Schörner 2012

G. Schörner. Comparing Surface, Topsoil and Subsurface Ceramic Assemblages: the Case of Il Monte, San Gimignano, in: G. Schörner – P. Attema (eds.), Comparative Issues in the Archaeology of the Roman Rural Landscape: Site Classification between Survey, Excavation and Historical Categories (Portsmouth 2012).

Semple 1932

E. C. Semple, The Geography of the Mediterranean Region: Its Relation to Ancient History (London 1932).

Spruyt 1994

H. Spruyt, The Sovereign State and Its Competitors: an Analysis of Systems Change (Princeton 1994).

Terrenato 2000

N. Terrenato, The Visibility of Sites and the Interpretation of Field Survey Results: Towards an Analysis of Incomplete Distributions, in: R. Francovich – H. Patterson (eds.), Extracting Meaning from Ploughsoil Assemblages (Oxford 2000).

Terrenato 2012

N. Terrenato, The Essential Countryside: the Roman World, in: S. E. Alcock – R. Osborne, Classical Archaeology ^{2}(Chichester 2012).

Tol et al. 2014

G. Tol – T. de Haas – K. Armstrong – P. Attema. Minor Centres in the Pontine Plain: the Case of Forum Appii and Ad Medias, BSR 82, 2014, 109–134.

van Dommelen – Finocchi 2008

P. van Dommelen – S. Finocchi, Sardinia: Diverging Landscapes, in: P. van Dommelen – C. Gómez Bellard (eds.), Rural Landscapes of the Punic World (London 2008).

van Dommelen et al. 2008

P. van Dommelen – A. S. Giammellaro – F. Spatafora, Sicily and Malta: between Sea and Countryside, in: P. van Dommelen – C. Gómez Bellard (eds.), Rural Landscapes of the Punic World (London 2008).

van Dommelen – Gómez Bellard 2008

P. van Dommelen – C. Gómez Bellard, Conclusion, in: P. van Dommelen – C. Gómez Bellard (eds.), Rural Landscapes of the Punic World (London 2008).

Witcher 2006

R. Witcher, Broken Pots and Meaningless Dots? Surveying the Rural Landscapes of Roman Italy, BSR 74, 2006, 39–72.

Witcher 2012
R. Witcher. 'That from a Long Way off Look like Farms': the Classification of Roman Rural Sites, in: P. Attema – G. Schörner, Comparative Issues in the Archaeology of the Roman Rural Landscape: Site Classification between Survey, Excavation and Historical Categories (Portsmouth 2012).

Yntema 1993
D. Yntema, In Search of an Ancient Countryside: the Amsterdam Free University Field Survey at Oria, Province of Brindisi, South Italy (1981–1983) (Amsterdam 1993).

Measuring Rural Economic Development through Categorical Data Analysis in Southern Etruria and Latium (400 BC–50 AD)

Stephen A. Collins-Elliott

Abstract

The comparison of the results of rural surveys and excavations has been a long-standing interest in the study of the ancient economy, seeking above all a way to measure changes in settlement patterns and site hierarchies over time. Nevertheless, cross-comparison has been inhibited by numerous factors, including differences in sample size, survey intensity, and classification. This paper presents practical techniques to address these issues, and focuses on the computational methodology employed to obtain estimates of the prevalence or degree of features in the landscape of southern Etruria and northern Latium that pertain to economic processes. As a proof-of-concept, it uses the published data from four survey projects around Caere, Fidenae, Crustumerium, and Cures Sabini (fig. 1). The method consists of a script, written in Python, that automates the process of translating across categories, which works as follows.

First, classification is addressed using a flexible semantic concordance to standardize site- and artifact-level features from published surveys and excavations as an ontology, by which I mean a formal set of definitions and their relationships to one another, taking the form of a network. Linking concepts together provides a map of the associations that artifact and feature labels have with one another, affording an expedient means to rework different taxonomic systems. Thus, not only can cross-project concordances be standardized, but their semantic connotations can be explored beyond the confines of their definitions, relating sites to variable economic tasks and domains of life. For example, villas, emblematic of aristocratic rural life, are also loci of production, and defining an ontology which links these categories together can serve to accommodate these overlapping associations. Second, the estimation of the prevalence of selected categorical factors can then proceed using random subsampling. This involves taking a random sample from the observed sample of sites, of a smaller size than the actual sample, to address the known factor of loss in the archaeological record and assess the quality of the data for how it varies in its size, which is reflective of the intensity of collection. Uncertainty is thereby accommodated within the estimation of different categorical features in the landscape of the Tiber River Valley.

Thus, it is possible to provide a more accurate assessment of quantified, long-term change in the rural economy, as the population of Rome increased over the last several centuries BC and first half of the first century AD. It is suggested that regional development in the *suburbium* is uneven, and certain phenomena might not be necessarily linked, such as the proliferation of large villas and the use of amphora-borne commodities (whether production or consumption). Further work to examine patterns of association, whether using methods like correspondence analysis, non-metric multidimensional scaling, and/or correlation, will be necessary. But, the practical tools developed here are aimed at moving toward a multi-faceted perspective of economic development and integration in the countryside beyond site counts and the intensity of agricultural productivity.

Introduction

The comparison of rural surveys has been a subject of continued interest in the study of the Roman *suburbium,* seeking above all a way to measure changes in settlement patterns and site hierarchies over time.[1] The issues have been long-discussed within the framework of project restudy, resurveying, and cross-project synthesis.[2] Where the aim of regional analysis has been the quantification of sites, finds, and the estimation of their surface density, the most ostensible culprits which impede straightforward comparison are differential visibility factors, methodology, and the intensity of fieldwork.[3] Different systems of classification also pose a significant problem, since different terms may be applied to identical finds or site-types, and vice-versa.[4] The representativeness of surface finds to those from subsurface strata is particular to the formation processes of each site. To be sure, this is ancillary to the larger (and unanswerable) question of the quantitative relationship of assemblages to the material culture in actual use in the past.[5] However, finding measures of rural economic development can profit from computational methods, not just in dealing with the uncertainty and doubt surrounding quantitative data, but also in interpretation and classification. This paper presents an approach as a proof-of-concept, to measure the prevalence of different categorical attributes or features within a landscape over time.

This paper proceeds in two sections. First, I outline a computational method to expedite the reclassification of archaeological finds, features, and site-types. Second, I implement a method of resampling to obtain statistical information on the estimations of the prevalence of different features.

Archaeological Classification and Semantic Networks

To start, it should be noted that the act of collecting finds and recording sites is not akin to an empirical trial, where a hypothesis is put forward, tested, and either proven or disproved. Rather, it comprises the accumulation of descriptive observations of conditions which are well beyond the control of the investigator. In synthesizing data from different projects, the lowest common denominator can be viewed as the factors of presence and "pseudo-absence" (since it is impossible to confirm absence) at a given location. The use of what might be called low-quality or low-resolution data can find some parallels in ecological studies of species detection, which employ presence and presence-absence data in conjunction with geographic data to produce predictive maps.[6] While predictive analysis is not the aim here, basic factors of presence and pseudo-absence provide a useful foundation toward the comparison of the regional distribution of features in the landscape. Each site can be considered in terms of its categorical attributes or features (such as its finds assemblages and other denotative qualities), whose presence can be indicated with either a yes (1) or a no (0).

Comparison mandates that the same definitions should be employed for every site. Nevertheless, archaeologists have yet to establish discipline-wide classificatory standards, and even if such standardization could be achieved, one would still have to deal with the task of reconciling past classificatory systems. The solution lies in creating an effective means of translating across projects. To that end, a semantic network provides a useful summary representation of the relationship between different concepts, as an ontology.[7] The ontology developed for this paper was drawn from the terminology employed in four well-known surveys in southern Etruria and northern Latium, listed in Table 1.

These explicit terms were supplemented with connotative associations that extended to larger behavioral domains (as broadly as "domestic" or "economic"), as well as translations from Italian into English. The sum of terms in the ontology came to 365, and

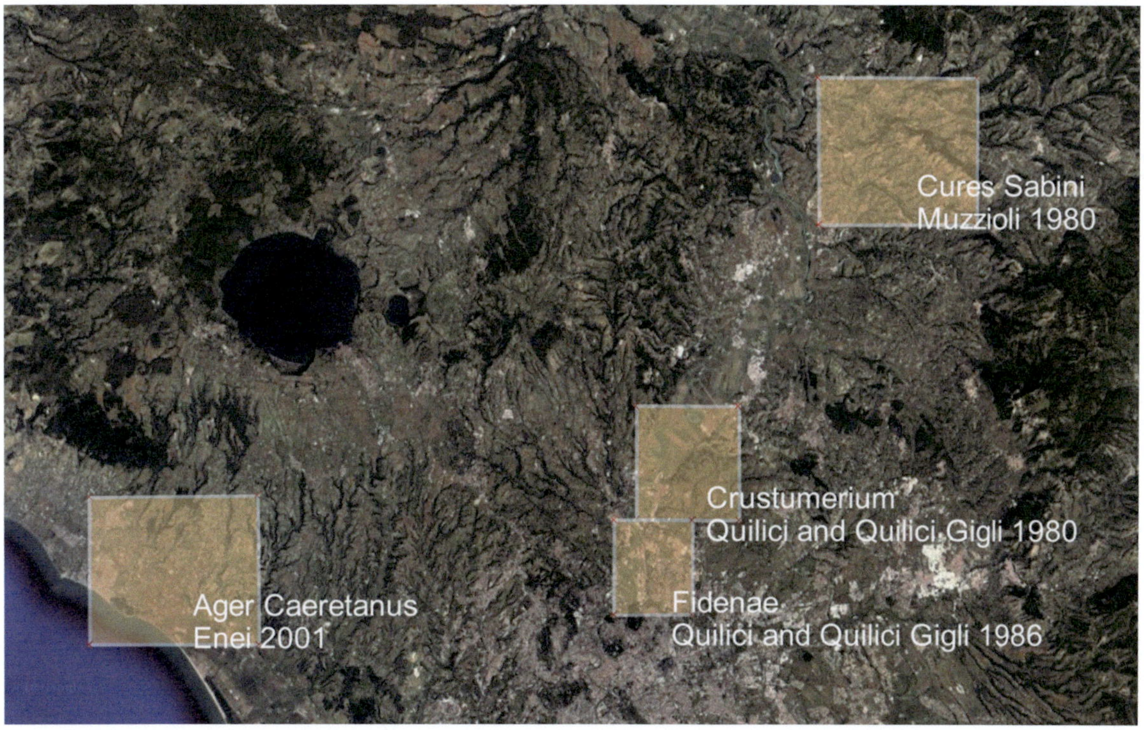

Fig. 1: Boundaries of the survey regions listed in Table 1.

Region	*N*	Publication
Ager Caeretanus	91	Enei 2001.
Crustumerium	128	Quilici – Quilici Gigli 1980.
Cures Sabini	139	Muzzioli 1980.
Fidenae	36	Quilici – Quilici Gigli 1986.

Table 1: Published surveys in south Etruria and northern Latium which provided data for this project, illustrated in Figure 1. *N* represents the number of sites in each sample set (not the total number of sites in the survey publication).

in the interest of keeping the ontology simple, relationships were kept at the level of "implies," through a directed line (fig. 2). For example, a string of relationships can be traced through the following links, with each feature in brackets:

[loomweight] ⟶ [textile production] ⟶ [craft production] ⟶ [economic]

The full network and all data are available online.[8] It should be noted that this network is under development, and, to be sure, alternative ontologies should be implemented to test for categorical stability or consistency.

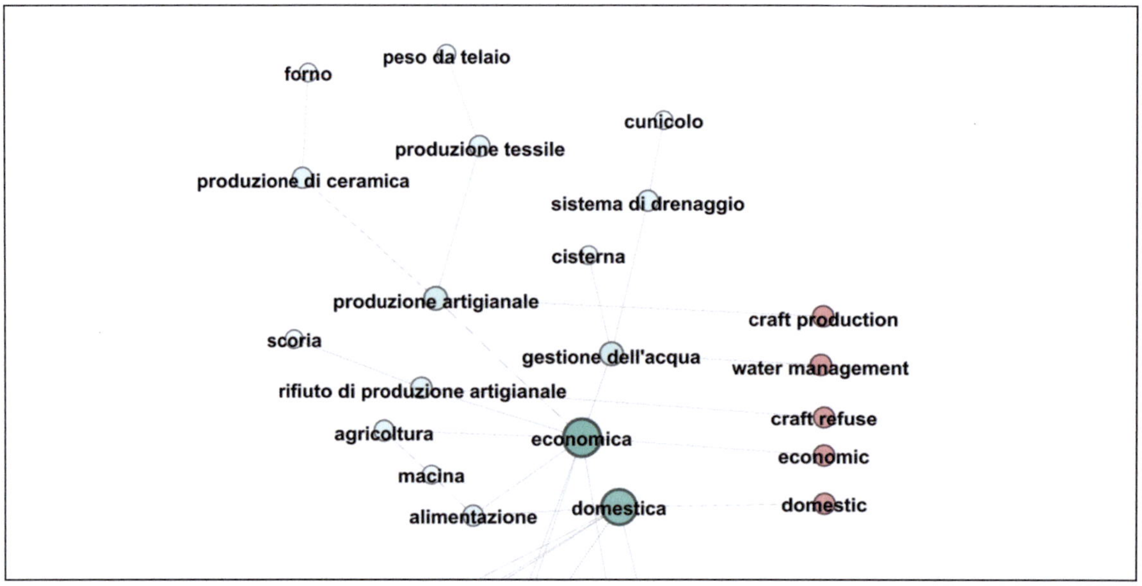

Fig. 2: Partial section of the semantic network showing links between associated concepts. Terms were left in Italian for the sake of convenience, with English translations added where necessary.

A partial set of site descriptions from each of these projects was then collected, breaking down each entry into its constituted set of features. For example, we can take the entry for site no. 268 from the *Ager Caeretanus* project:[9]

> 268. Area di frammenti
> Ampia circa 900 mq con densità 2, su terreno arpicato, di formazione alluvionale molto recente, coltivato a vignetto. Si rivengono: impasto rosso-bruno (*pithoi*, olle, bacini), sigillata italica (f. XXXVII), sigillata africana (prod. D), anfore (f. Will A/C, Dressel 2/4), comune imperiale da fuoco; tegole di I° fase, tegole romane, numerose scaglie calcaree e tufacee.
> Presenze di epoca etrusca (VII?–VI sec. a.C.) e romana (III sec. a.C.; I–IV sec. d.C.).
> Cerveteri, Casalone di Ceri, 10.8.88 (tav. 40).

The description can be recast into a set of features, with its phases listed as sets of intervals ("[−300,−200]" being the equivalent of the third century BC), coded in JSON:[10]

```
{
"id": "268",
"dates": ["[-300,-200]", "[1,400]"],
"features": ["area di frammenti", "sigillata italica",
    "Will A-C", "Dressel 2-4", "comune imperiale da fuoco",
    "tegola", "scaglie calcaree",
    "scaglie tufacee"]
}
```

Characteristics like scatter size could be added to the feature list. Features can also be coded with a dating phase, in order to avoid chronological contamination: E.g., [sigillata italica] can be assigned the date range [−30,75], or [comune imperiale da fuoco] the date range [−30,300]. Moreover, that attribute can be more precisely labeled as [comune imperiale da fuoco, Enei 2001], in order to avoid conflicting with an identical ceramic class from another project which might have a different periodization.[11] That said, superfluous attributes do not need to be added, for example, [amphora], since that vessel class is implicit in the finds of Greco-Italic (Will A-C) and Dressel 2-4 amphorae at the site. The script I wrote in Python returned a value of "1" if the feature was present at that site for a given year, and "0" if it was missing (pseudo-absent) from the site (Tab. 2).

The Python script then ran through the semantic network to see if any of the features present could be related to an attribute in question, translating that feature into all possible associated terms. Thus, specifying a feature like [amphora] would return the total sum of sites in the specific period which had attested any amphora class; specifying "craft production" yielded the total number of sites which had any features related to

	−250	50
area di frammenti	1	1
sigillata italica	0	1
Will A-C	1	0
Dressel 2-4	0	1
comune imp. da fuoco	0	1
tegola	1	1
scaglie calcaree	1	1
scaglie tufacee	1	1

Table 2: Presence/pseudo-absence table for the years ca. 250 BCE and 50 CE, using the example of *Ager Caeretanus* project, site no. 268, from Enei 2001, 201.

any type of craftwork (for example, loomweights, kilns). This represents the simplest form that such an ontology could take, given the variety of possible relationships. More elaborate and hierarchical networks would provide more nuanced ways of construing archaeological definitions and their associations. In sum, by transferring the interpretive process of archaeological artifacts to the formal ontology, a rapid means of reclassification is achieved, and any issues with the system of definitions and classes can be dealt with by reworking the ontology.

Subsampling Estimation

Proceeding to the second part of the paper, I estimate the prevalence of any one of these features using the total sum of sites as the population, rather than the surface area of the region in question. The object of estimation is therefore not counts of sites, but rather the proportion of sites that possessed a given feature in a region. It is also desirable to obtain information about the strength of certainty in the those estimates. Even as the population (the total number of sites) is unknown, we can nevertheless be sure that a portion of the total sites that were once occupied have been detected. Accordingly, a process of simulation that resamples from our sample would appear to be the most effective means to get information about variance, and hence a credible interval that would indicate the upper and lower boundaries of the measure according to a given level of certainty. While the bootstrap (resampling the same sample size with replacement) has been a popular technique, the premise of information loss would suggest that subsampling with a smaller sample size might be more germane to the situation of the archaeological data, and is worth exploring.[12]

This process of random subsampling simulates the effects of alternative results, where one has detected even fewer sites than what are in the sample. The script in Python accordingly selected a random subsample from the list of sites, and calculated the frequency of a given feature over a number of simulated runs (here, 1,000). The resulting set of simulated values could then be used to construct a probability density to locate the most probable value, argmax(x), as well as other descriptive statistics.[13] A histogram of subsampled values and the probability density derived from those subsamples are given in an example in Figure 3, which shows the probable estimation of the frequency of features of [amphora] and [water management] (the presence of a cistern or any system of channels), in the *Forma Italiae* survey around Cures Sabini.[14] With a certainty interval of 85%, the value of the subsampled frequency of amphorae lies between 0.18 and 0.50. According to the same degree of certainty, the subsampled frequency of features related to water management can be located within the range of 0.00 and 0.21. It can also be noted that a number of zero values will emerge in the course of subsampling, which could be taken as null values: one solution to this tendency is to construct the density on the open interval (0,1), which would exclude the values of 0 and 1. Similar spikes may be found at common fractional intervals, such as 0.5, 0.33, and 0.66: in the case of an overly small sample (such as only three or four sites), these

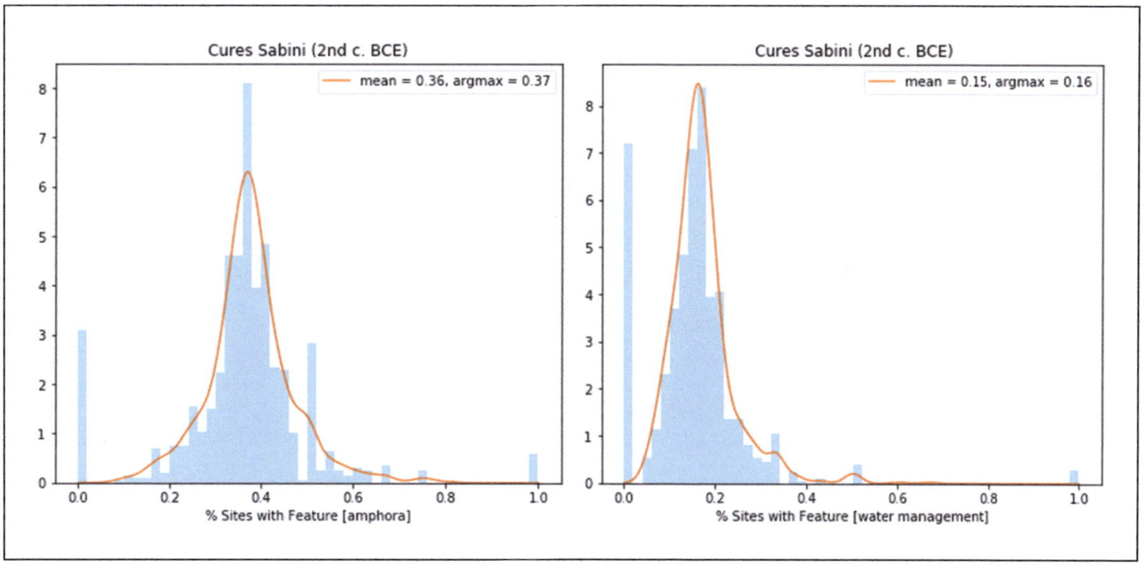

Fig. 3: Histograms and densities on the interval (0,1) of the subsampled values for the *Forma Italiae* survey around Cures Sabini for two different features, ca. 150 BC. Values of the mean and argmax (value which had the highest probability) in upper right-hand corner.

values may be the only ones which are generated by the subsampling routine, which would be clear in the histograms of the subsampling estimates.

This approach, which makes no assumptions about the shape of the data (i.e., that it would follow a normal distribution), is fruitful in that it allows for information on the effects of the sample size (the number of sites observed) to be carried over into a probability density. This can be used in constructing more complex models of the ancient economy. Rather than having a fixed or assumed *ad hoc* value, probability densities can provide a more nuanced picture about the degree to which we can be sure about our quantitative data.

To conclude with a few examples, it is important to highlight that the above procedure has its limits with the published data. It is not possible, for example, to ask questions about craft refuse or waste (as in the form of metal slag) from the survey around Fidenae, because that material class was not described in the survey catalogue. Other surveys might have been more thorough in the consistency with which they noted or labeled finds. That said, some classes of features or site-types remain valid. To take the features of [amphora], [villa], and [craft production] into consideration, the subsampled estimates of the prevalence of each feature can be plotted over time using a jitterplot, showing which values have a higher probability given the clustering of points (fig. 4).

To look at the case of one artifact class, amphorae, it might not be possible to compare frequencies across projects if they do not note their presence with the same regularity. However, assuming that the surveys are at least somewhat internally consistent, it should be possible to compare trends. In the case of the prevalence of amphorae, then, there would appear to be no clear pattern visible over time: both the *Ager Caeretanus* project and the *Forma Italiae* Cures Sabini survey show a peak, but at different moments of time. Around Caere the peak occurs in the first century BC, while around Cures Sabini it occurs around the second century BC. Crustumerium returns fairly consistently low frequencies of sites with amphorae, while the data from Fidenae appear to warrant little confidence for establishing a clear pattern before the second century BC, given the dispersion of the subsamples. There would at least seem to be a measure of micro-regional variation in the Roman *suburbium,* in either the production of amphorae or the transport and use of amphora-borne commodities.

There is, however, a more apparent trend in the prevalence of villas, a site-type which has been of long-standing use in the field, even as there is a movement away to the prescriptive archetype of the "Catonian" villa toward a recognition of the architectural variety which large rural estates had in the period of the Roman Republic.[15] Notwithstanding the assumed definition of villas, their prevalence in the landscape seems to undergo a steady increase into the last several centuries BC and first century AD in all but one of the survey regions, Cures Sabini. The exceedingly high frequency of villas (around 50% of the total number of sites) approaches that of the *Ager Cosanus,* a region recognized to have had one of the highest densities of villas in Etruria.[16] In light of this observation, it would be a fruitful exercise to revisit the construction of the concept of

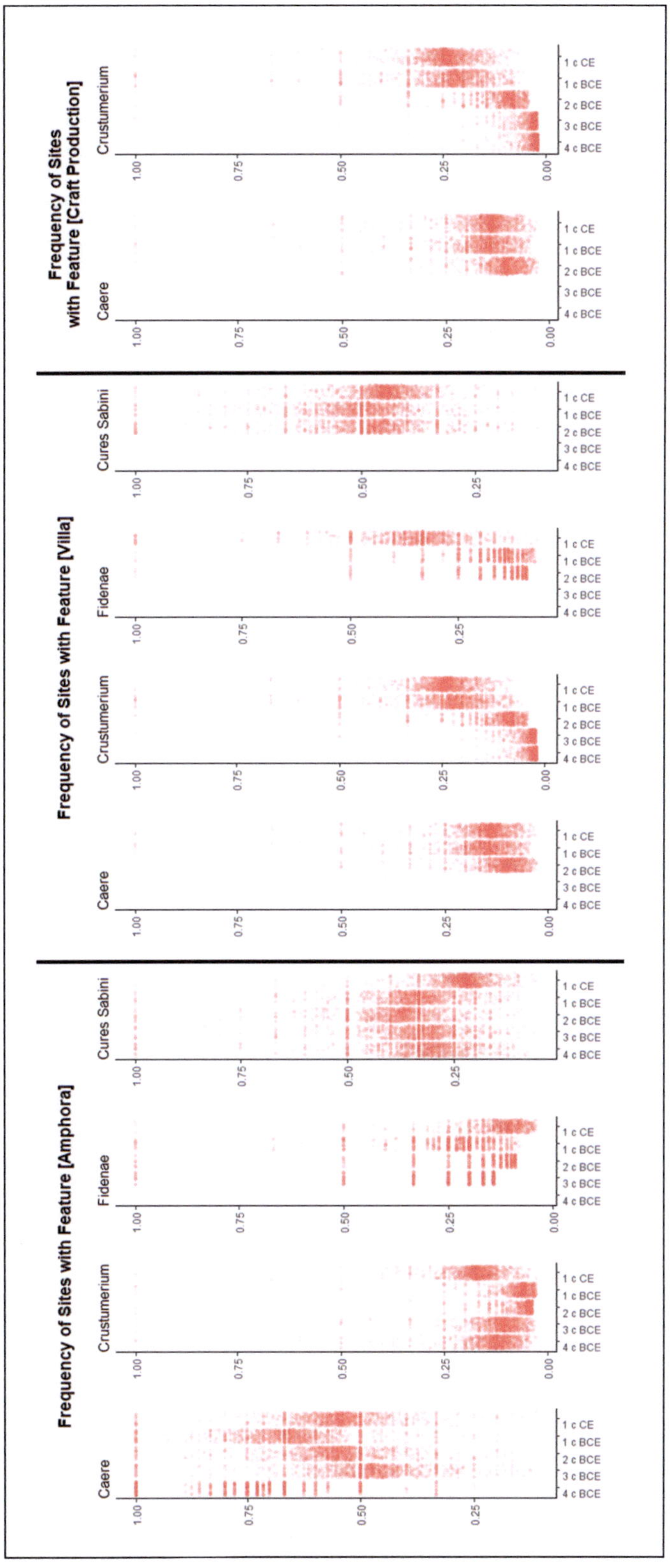

Fig. 4: Jitterplots of the subsampled frequency of select features in four south Etrurian/northern Latial landscapes, ca. 400 BC–50 AD: amphorae, villas, and craft production.

"villa" through the semantic network and to fully explore the range of connotations which the attendant material culture and architectural features has for its definition. Evaluating the correlation between the frequency of sites with amphorae (potentially as an indicator of maritime or riverine connectivity) and villas, and the relationship with other categories of evidence would also be useful, since these trends do not appear to be connected with one another.

Beyond either the artifact-type or the site-type, the use of a semantic network can expedite the process of measuring abstract indices, such as craft production, in the landscape. By linking material finds related to the production of textiles, ceramics, glass, and iron to a node in the network labeled [craft production], any finds which fell under that classification were automatically assigned that label. The results however can only be generated for two out of the four surveys, those around Caere and Crustumerium, while Fidenae and Cures Sabini lacked any evidence which pertained to those activities. They nevertheless would appear to show a gradual increase in the number of rural sites where craft activities were taking place, from the third-second century BC (around Caere) into the first century AD. However, comparing the prevalence of different features over time shows that not all categories of evidence work, due to the focus of interest in each survey (as in the case of craft refuse noted above).

Conclusions

Further data are necessary before proceeding with firm conclusions about the development of the rural economy in the hinterland of Rome over the last several centuries BC. Nevertheless, these preliminary results indicate that economic developments within the *suburbium* are not uniform or homogenous over the last four centuries BC and first century AD. The methods developed here also illustrate that inter-regional comparisons can be achieved computationally, both to expedite the translation of features across projects and to accommodate uncertainty in their quantification. There are a number of issues which impact site recovery rates and material culture in attendance, from visibility to the sampling strategies employed. Yet, the premise that there is a certain amount of information loss in the observation of archaeological data provides motivation for randomized subsampling as a means to simulate statistical information, which can serve to provide credibility in estimation. In turn, probability densities can be resampled and incorporated into more complex models of the ancient economy, allowing for a more accurate picture of the certainty or uncertainty of conclusions.

Looking ahead, the economic development of the *suburbium* (and beyond) can be measured not merely for increases or decreases in the numbers of sites occupied and the distribution of specific artifact-types, but for the prevalence of broader factors, like craft production, whose relationship to finds and site-types can be related through a semantic network. The use of random subsampling can be used to transfer the effects of sample size onto estimates, and further to establish probability densities for incorporation to more complex models of economic interaction. This approach enables the easy manipulation of classificatory schemes as well as a means to obtain summary statistics on estimates with an unknown population. It constitutes a basis for multivariate methods of categorical data analysis that can examine the relationships among multiple factors at work, involving correlation, multidimensional scaling, principal component analysis, and multiple correspondence analysis, to assess the dynamics of economic relationships at work in the countryside.

Notes

[1] Witcher 2005a; Witcher 2005b; Witcher 2006; Patterson et al. 2004. For the impact of the growth of the city of Rome on its hinterland, see Morley 1996.

[2] In general, see papers in Francovich – Patterson 2000; Alcock – Cherry 2004; Attema – Schörner 2012.

[3] Cherry 1983; Shennan 1985; Terrenato – Ammerman 1996; Banning 2002, 46–49. 60–68; Bintliff 2002; Terrenato 2004.

[4] Witcher 2012.

[5] Haselgrove 1985; Schörner 2012.

[6] Manel et al. 2001; Ferrier et al. 2002; Brotons et al. 2004; Phillips et al. 2006; Liu et al. 2011. On predictive analysis in the Tiber river valley see Kay – Witcher 2009.

[7] Quillian 1967; see Calvanese et al. 2016; Collins-Elliott 2018. Brughmans 2010; Brughmans 2013 discuss the development of formal network approaches in archaeology with previous bibliography.

[8] The project files are available from the repository at <http://www.github.com/scollinselliott/tyrrhenian/> (23.09.2018).

[9] Enei 2001, 201 no. 268.

[10] The original script in python relied on csv tables for both the datasets and the semantic network. These have been converted into json for downloading.

[11] For automated taxonomic concordances in dealing with ceramics, see Collins-Elliott 2016.

[12] Baxter 2003, 148–154; key works on the bootstrap and the related technique of the jackknife include Miller 1974; Efron 1979; Efron – Tibshirani 1994. Formal treatment of subsampling can be found in Politis – Romano 1994; Politis et al. 1999.

[13] On kernel density estimation see Baxter 2003, 30–33.

[14] Muzzioli 1980.

[15] See Terrenato 2001; Marzano 2007, 3–5; Terrenato 2007; and papers in Becker – Terrenato 2012.

[16] Carandini et al. 2002; Witcher 2006, 93 Tab. 1.

Image Credits

All images by the author.

References

Alcock – Cherry 2004
S. Alcock – J. Cherry (eds.), Side-by-Side Survey. Comparative Regional Studies in the Mediterranean World (Oxford 2004).

Attema – Schörner 2012
P. Attema – G. Schörner (eds.), Comparative Issues in the Archaeology of the Roman Rural Landscape. Site Classification Between Survey, Excavation and Historical Categories, JRA Suppl. 88 (Portsmouth 2012).

Banning 2002
E. Banning, Archaeological Survey (New York 2002).

Baxter 2003
M. Baxter, Statistics in Archaeology (London 2003).

Becker – Terrenato 2012
J. Becker – N. Terrenato (eds.), Roman Republican Villas: Architecture, Context, and Ideology (Ann Arbor 2012).

Bintliff 2002
J. Bintliff, Settlement Pattern Analysis and Demographic Modeling, in: P. Attema – G.-J. Burgers – E. van Joolen – M. van Leusen – B. Mater (eds.), New Developments in Italian Landscape Archaeology (Oxford 2002) 28–35.

Brotons et al. 2004
L. Brotons – W. Thuiller – M. Araújo – A. Hirtzel, Presence–absence versus Presence-only. Modelling Methods for Predicting Bird Habitat Suitability, Ecography 27, 2004, 437–448.

Brughmans 2010
T. Brughmans, Connecting the Dots: towards Archaeological Network Analysis, OxfJA 2010, 2010, 277–303.

Brughmans 2013
T. Brughmans, Thinking Through Networks: A Review of Formal Network Methods in Archaeology, AMethTh 20, 2013, 623–662.

Calvanese et al. 2016
D. Calvanese – P. Liuzzo – A. Mosca – J. Remesal – M. Rezk – G. Rull, Ontology-based Data Integration in EPNet: Production and Distribution of Food during the Roman Empire, Engineering Applications of Artificial Intelligence 51, 2016, 212–229.

Carandini et al. 2002
A. Carandini – M. Celuzza – E. Fentress – I. Attolini (ed.), Paesaggi d'Etruria. Valle dell'Albegna, Valle d'Oro, Valle del Chiarone, Valle del Tafone (Rome 2002).

Cherry 1983
J. Cherry, Frogs around the Pond: Perspectives on Current Archaeological Survey Projects in the Mediterranean Area, in: D. Keller – D. Rupp (ed.), Archaeological Survey in the Mediterranean Area, BARIntSer 155 (Oxford 1983) 375–416.

Collins-Elliott 2016
S. Collins-Elliott, Agglomerative Clustering Using Cosine and Jaccard Distances: A Computational Approach to Roman Vessel Taxonomy, ACalc 27, 2016, 7–25.
Collins-Elliott 2018
S. Collins-Elliott, A Behavioral Analysis of Monetary Exchange and Craft Production in Rural Tuscany via Small Finds from the Roman Peasant Project, JMedA 31, 2018, 155–179.
Efron 1979
B. Efron, Bootstrap Methods: Another Look at the Jackknife, The Annals of Statistics 7, 1979, 1–26.
Efron – Tibshirani 1994
B. Efron – R. Tibshirani, An Introduction to the Bootstrap (Boca Raton 1994).
Enei 2001
F. Enei, Progetto Ager Caeretanus. Il litorale di Alsium (Ladispoli 2001).
Ferrier et al. 2002
S. Ferrier – G. Watson – J. Pearce – M. Drielsma, Extended Statistical Approaches to Modelling Spatial Pattern in Biodiversity in Northeast New South Wales 1. Species-level modelling, Biodiversity and Conservation 11, 2002, 2275–2307.
Francovich – Patterson 2000
R. Francovich – H. Patterson (eds.), Extracting Meaning from Ploughsoil Assemblages, The Archaeology of Mediterranean Landscapes 5 (Oxford 2000).
Haselgrove 1985
C. Haselgrove, Inference from Ploughsoil Artefact Samples, in: C. Haselgrove – C. Millet – I. Smith (eds.), Archaeology from the Ploughsoil: Studies in the Collection and Interpretation of Field Survey Data (Sheffield 1985) 7–29.
Kay – Witcher 2009
S. Kay – R. Witcher, Predictive Modelling of Roman Settlement in the Middle Tiber Valley, ACalc 20, 2009, 277–290.
Liu et al. 2011
C. Liu – M. White – G. Newell, Measuring and Comparing the Accuracy of Species Distribution Models with Presence-absence Data, Ecography 34, 2011, 232–243.
Manel et al. 2001
S. Manel – H. Williams – S. Ormerod, Evaluating Presence–absence Models in Ecology: the Need to Account for Prevalence, Journal of Applied Ecology 38, 2001, 921–931.
Marzano 2007
A. Marzano, Roman Villas in Central Italy: A Social and Economic History (Leiden 2007).
Miller 1974
R. Miller, The Jackknife – A Review, Biometrika 61, 1974, 1–15.
Morley 1996
N. Morley, Metropolis and Hinterland: The City of Rome and the Italian Economy, 200 BC–AD 200 (Cambridge 1996).
Muzzioli 1980
M. Muzzioli, Cures Sabini, Forma Italiae Regio IV – Vol. II (Florence 1980).

Patterson et al. 2004
H. Patterson – H. Di Giuseppe – R. Witcher, Three South Etrurian 'Crises': First Results of the Tiber Valley Project, BSR 72, 2004, 1–36.
Phillips et al. 2006
S. Phillips – R. Anderson – R. Schapire, Maximum Entropy Modeling of Species Geographic Distributions, Ecological Modelling 190, 2006, 231–259.
Politis – Romano 1994
D. Politis – J. Romano, Large Sample Confidence Regions Based on Subsamples under Minimal Assumptions, The Annals of Statistics 22, 1994, 2031–2050.
Politis et al. 1999
D. Politis – J. Romano – M. Wolf, Subsampling (New York 1999).
Quilici – Quilici Gigli 1980
L. Quilici – S. Quilici Gigli, Crustumerium, Latium Vetus 3 (Rome 1980).
Quilici – Quilici Gigli 1986
L. Quilici – S. Quilici Gigli, Fidenae, Latium Vetus 5 (Rome 1986).
Quillian 1967
M. Quillian, Word Concepts: a Theory and Simulation of Some Basic Semantic Capabilities, Behavioral Science 12, 1967, 410–430.
Schörner 2012
G. Schörner, Comparing Surface, Topsoil and Subsurface Ceramic Assemblages: the Case of Il Monte, San Gimignano, in: P. Attema – G. Schörner (eds.), Comparative Issues in the Archaeology of the Roman Rural Landscape. Site Classification Between Survey, Excavation and Historical Categories, JRA Suppl. 88 (Portsmouth 2012) 31–41.
Shennan 1985
S. Shennan, Experiments in the Collection and Analysis of Archaeological Survey Data: The East Hampshire Survey (Sheffield 1985).
Terrenato 2001
N. Terrenato, The Auditorium Site in Rome and the Origins of the villa, JRA 14, 2001, 5–32.
Terrenato 2004
N. Terrenato, Sample Size Matters! The Paradox of Global Trends and Local Surveys, in: S. Alcock – J. Cherry (eds.), Side-by-Side Survey. Comparative Regional Studies in the Mediterranean World (Oxford 2004) 36–48.
Terrenato 2007
N. Terrenato, The Essential Countryside: The Roman World, in: S. Alcock – R. Osborne (eds.), Classical Archaeology (Malden 2007) 139–161.
Terrenato – Ammerman 1996
N. Terrenato – A. Ammerman, Visibility and Site Recovery in the Cecina Valley Survey, JFieldA 23, 1996, 91–109.
Witcher 2005a
R. Witcher, The Extended Metropolis: urbs, suburbium, and Population, JRA 19, 2005, 120–138.

Witcher 2005b
R. Witcher, The Hinterlands of Rome: Settlement Diversity in the Early Imperial Landscape of Regio VII Etruria., in: P. Attema – A. Nijboer – A. Zifferero (eds.), Papers in Italian Archaeology VI: Communities and Settlements from the Neolithic to the Early Medieval Period, BARIntSer 1452 (Oxford 2005) 1045–1055.

Witcher 2006
R. Witcher, Settlement and Society in Early Imperial Etruria, JRS 96, 2006, 88–123.

Witcher 2012
R. Witcher, 'That From A Long Way Off Look Like Farms': The Classification of Roman Rural Sites, in: P. Attema – G. Schörner (eds.), Comparative Issues in the Archaeology of the Roman Rural Landscape. Site Classification Between Survey, Excavation and Historical Categories, JRA Suppl. 88 (Portsmouth 2012) 11–30.

Towards an Integrated Database for the Study of Long-term Settlement Dynamics, Economic Performance and Demography in the Pontine Region and the Hinterland of Rome

Peter Attema – Tymon de Haas – Gijs Tol – Jorn Seubers

Introduction

For over 30 years, the Pontine Region Project (PRP) has carried out intensive archaeological artefact surveys in the Pontine region, a coastal landscape south of Rome (fig. 1). These surveys have resulted in a database holding site and ceramic data that derive from all the different landscape zones of this region, which include a coastal ridge, inland plain, volcanic hills, river valleys, foothills and surrounding mountain range. The PRP database structure is aimed at the aggregate and comparative analysis of rural settlement patterns across these different landscape zones in space and time, and to reconstruct economic and demographic trends on the local and regional scales from protohistory into the medieval period.

In the first part of this article we will give an overview of the challenges involved in creating this overarching project database, and present recent work done on the Pontine Region Project and its database as well as longitudinal socio-economic and demographic studies of the Pontine landscape and past populations to illustrate the analytical potential of data integration. So far, we have carried out a restricted number of quantified socio-economic case studies of specific landscapes within the Pontine Region[1] and are working towards truly comparative analyses on the regional scale of the Pontine landscape based on the Pontine data.[2] Moreover, we will outline an objective for the future: to incorporate 'legacy' datasets in our database. In our case these especially comprise topographic studies, among which are several Forma Italiae archaeological inventories to complement our own site data, and to allow us to link rural settlement patterns to urban development and infrastructure.[3]

In the second part of the paper, we discuss the possibility and potential to integrate the Pontine Region database with those of two other major survey projects, the Suburbium Project (Sapienza Rome) and the Tiber Valley Project (British School at Rome), to design an aggregate database that covers representative sections of Rome's *Suburbium*.[4] To this end, we have formed an international consortium of researchers from the Universities of Groningen (NL), Durham (UK), St. Andrews (UK), Cologne (G) and now also Leiden (NL) and Melbourne (AUS). This new project, called the Rome Hinterland Project (RHP), is supported by an internationalization grant from the Netherlands Organization of Scientific Research (NWO) to which all partners contributed financially.[5] This initiative will facilitate longitudinal and quantitative studies on socio-economic and demographic aspects of Rome's hinterland from its formation to well into the medieval period.

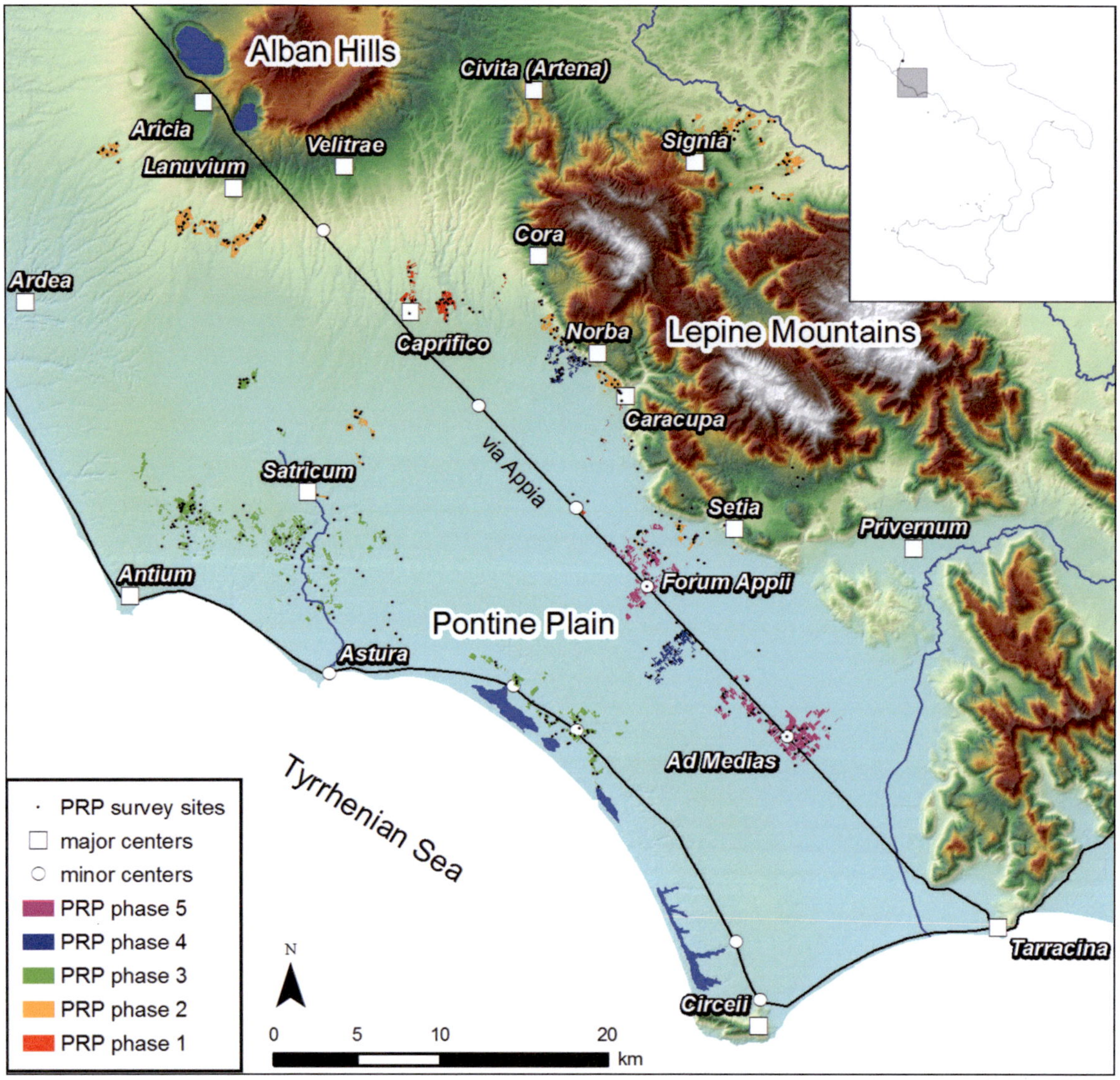

Fig. 1: The Pontine Region with areas and sites surveyed by the PRP.

The PRP Database: Highlighting the Potential for Quantitative Analyses

Thanks to the continuous collection of field data ever since its inception in 1987, the PRP database has grown into a rich but also complex source of archaeological data. Currently, it contains information on approximately 800 sites, 40 km^2 of off-site data and 300,000 artefacts, of which some 25,000 are diagnostic.[6] The dataset is complex because of the different methodologies that have been applied in our site and off-site surveys over the years. This was done for good reasons: we continuously wished to improve the quality of recording in the systematic survey of arable fields, to adapt our field methodology to survey of different terrain circumstances with low visibility (for instance in overgrown mountainous zones[7]), and to approach different research questions (which sometimes required the collection of off-site data, sometimes not). A challenge in extending the dataset is the incorporation of data collected in other projects carried out in the Pontine region, such as the Forma Italiae on Terracina and Circeii and their countryside;[8] Cora and its countryside;[9] and the Astura valley.[10] These inventories were compiled in a period when the archaeological landscape was far better preserved than today and therefore a crucial source to understand what we are currently able to map on the ground in much more fragmented form. To inventory these landscapes the topographers working in the Forma Italiae tradition used methods of field recording that are very different from the ones used today in Mediterranean survey. The surveys were extensive instead of intensive, more focused on the – then still abundantly present – standing monumental remains. Pottery was – if collected at all – usually taken as 'grab samples' instead of controlled pottery collections, and there was little or no attention given to quantitative ceramic analysis and off-site pottery recording. To make data from such older surveys ('legacy data') compatible with data captured by modern systematic survey, one must consider issues such as uneven coverage and research intensity; representation issues; uneven data quality and dating issues (to which we turn in the next paragraph).

To get a handle on the quality and significance of such topographic studies, resurveying sites they recorded is very useful.[11] This is clearly demonstrated by the resurveys done by the PRP in the early 2000s in the coastal landscape around Nettuno and along the Astura valley.[12] These resurveys allowed us to better understand the chronology and interpretation of sites mapped during earlier extensive non-systematic surveys in the area carried out for the Forma Italiae volume *Astura*[13] and by the then-Director of the Antiquarium of Nettuno. In addition, they focused on establishing scatter size, function, and site chronology. We integrated our own systematic survey with these enhanced data from extensive surveys to carry out settlement trend analysis,[14] as well as economic and demographic reconstructions.[15]

To illustrate this, fig. 2 shows the integration of the three datasets for the area around Nettuno (Piccareta's Forma Italiae volume, the Pontine Region dataset, and that of the Antiquarium at Nettuno) and the trends that can be derived from this aggregate dataset in terms of fluctuating rural occupation from the mid-Republic into the Imperial period. Such trends can be analysed in relation to the functioning of the Roman colony of Antium, and demonstrate that the fates of town and country were strongly tied, with both peaking in the Late Republican and Early Imperial periods. Once we have incorporated legacy datasets for other parts of the region, we will be able to perform such analyses on multiple scales, comparatively between towns and their rural territories or between landscape zones. These can even be done for more overarching aggregate socio-economic and demographic analyses concerning the rural history of the Pontine Region as a whole.

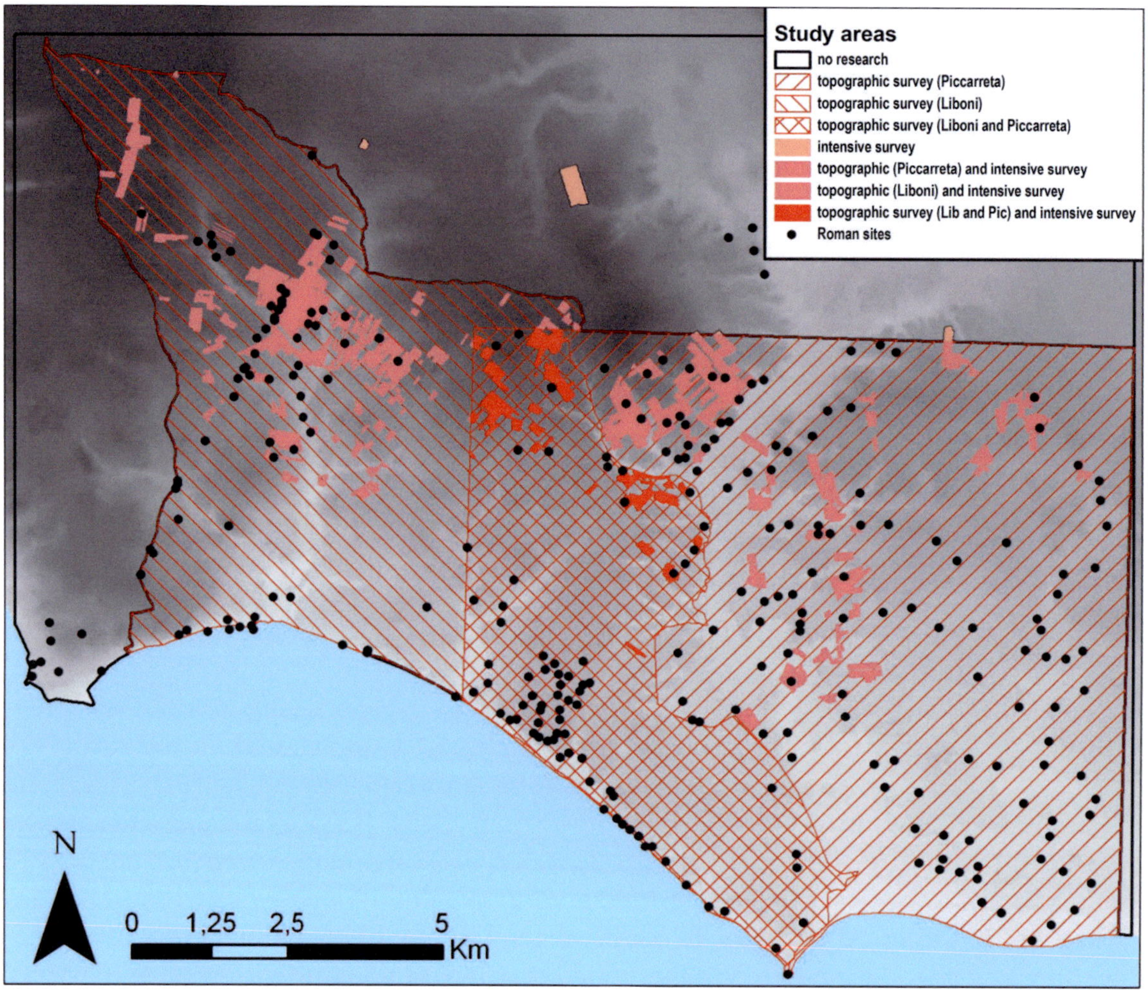

Fig. 2: Map showing three integrated, partially overlapping datasets.

Also, studies into economic performance and standard of living proved possible by combining our own field data with settlement- and artefactual information collected by the then-director of the Antiquarium of Nettuno. The graphs in figs. 3a, b show an example of how fine wares and amphorae can be used as indicators of access to and consumption of commodities in the countryside.[16] They show peaks in the late Republican and early Imperial periods. The building of the overarching PRP-database allows us to confront these local trends with those recorded for other parts of the Pontine region, teasing out differences in settlement and economic histories on the regional scale.[17] Analysing quantities of fine wares and amphorae at modest farmsteads and richer villas may show how far commodities reached the lower ends of the settlement spectrum, and hence if (and when) these were both economically integrated. Regarding the demographic inferences, we used the aggregated Nettuno data. Assigning numbers of persons to site classes and correcting numbers of sites for differential site recovery

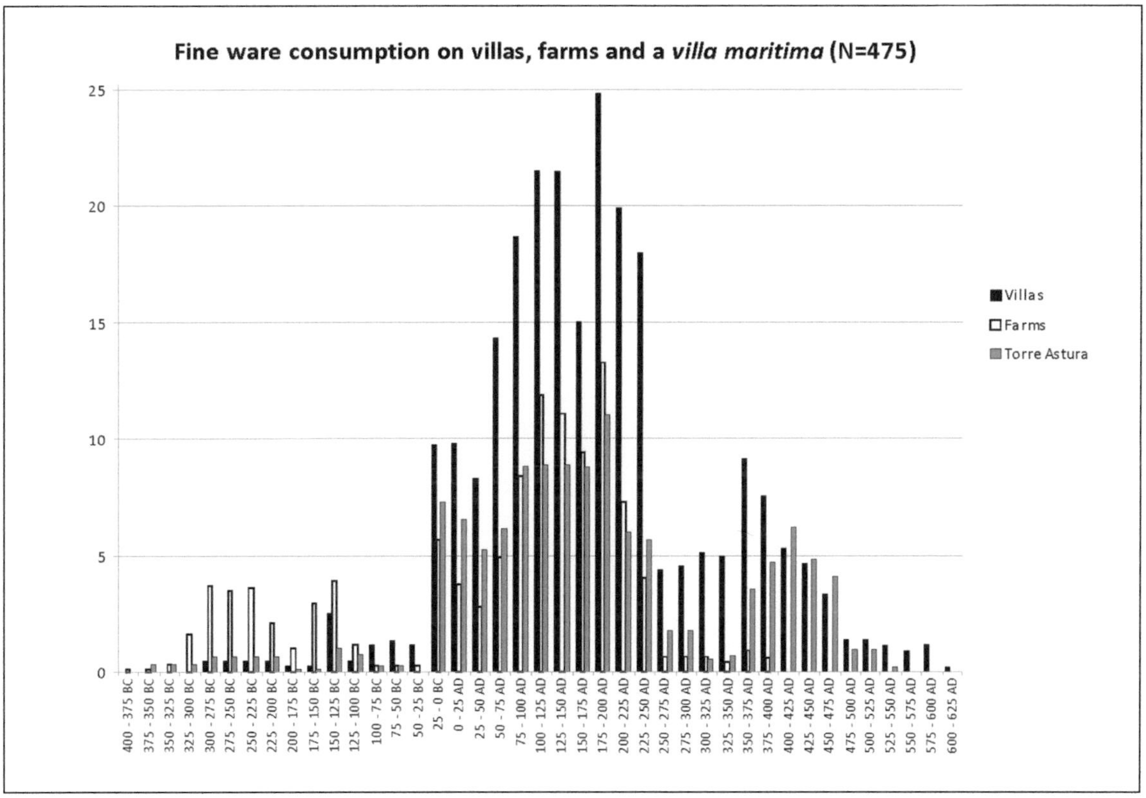

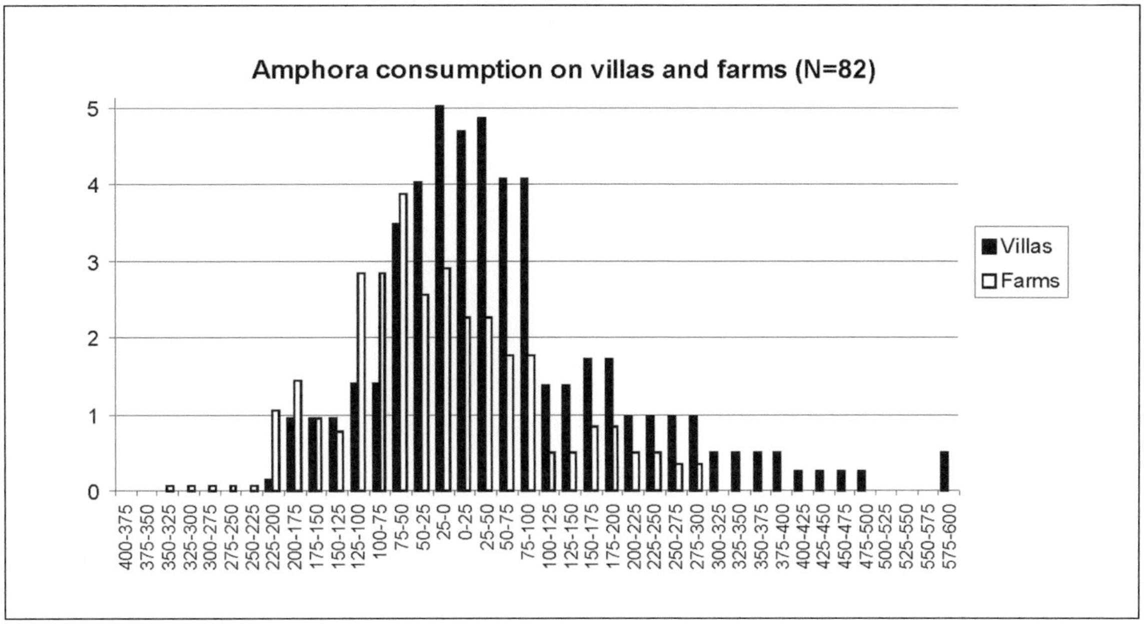

Fig. 3: 3a: Aggregated fine wares and amphorae for sites from a sample area in the Pontine region. 3b: Fine ware and amphora consumption between the 4th c. BC and 6th c. AD.

rates, we arrived at rural population estimates for the coastal landscape between *Satricum* and *Antium* for the Archaic to Roman periods.[18] We are convinced that, once we have added the vast amount of legacy data to the Pontine Region database, these studies will become more robust and will allow for comparisons over larger areas.

A third example of recent work on the PRP database is illustrated in fig. 4. It shows pottery production sites identified in the Pontine Region surveys from protohistory to the Roman period. In recent surveys we have been able to add to this sample, as geophysical surveys are now increasing the possibility of detecting actual kilns.[19] To reconstruct production and consumption patterns, as we are now endeavouring for the Pontine plain

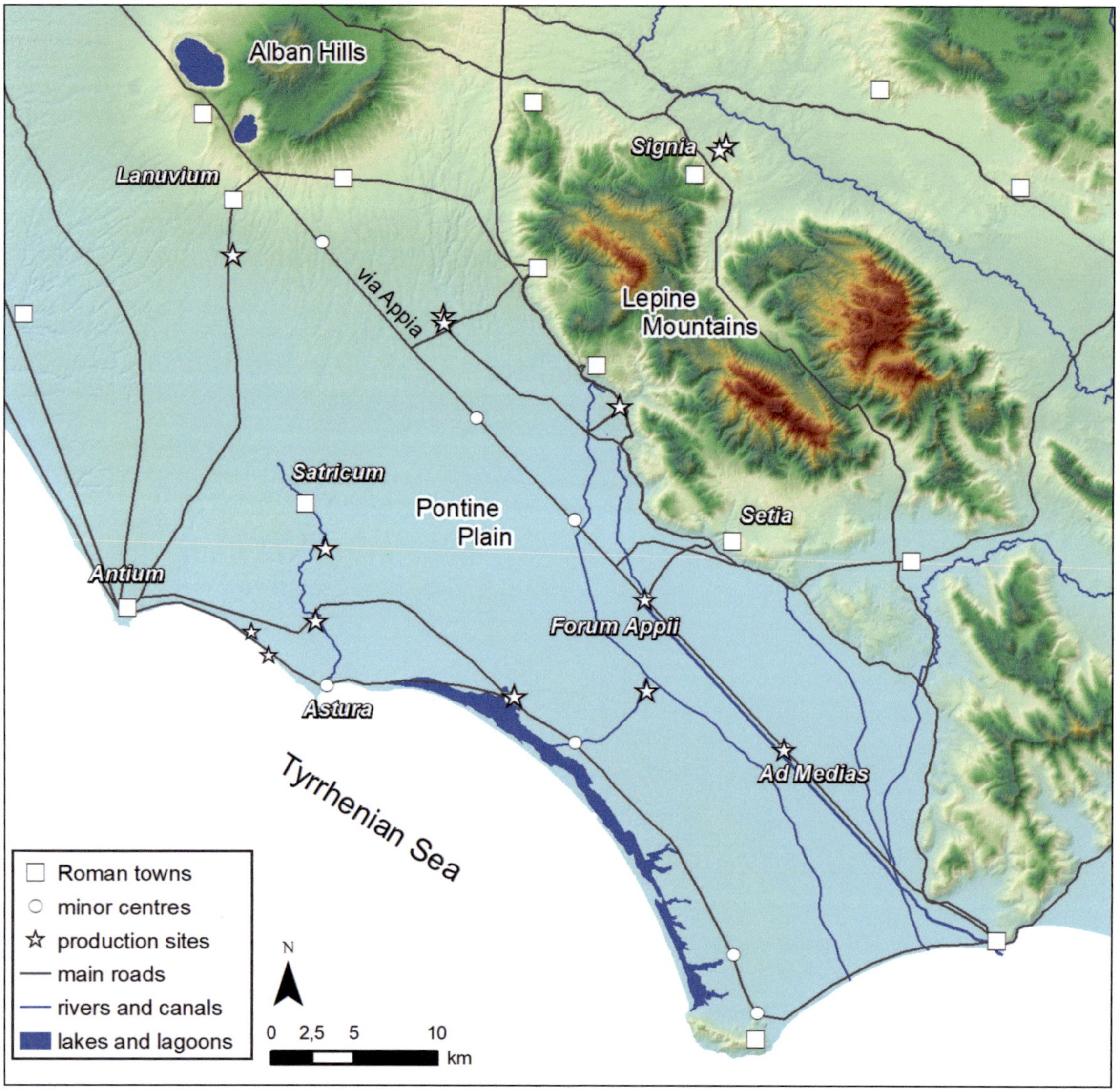

Fig. 4: Pottery production sites identified in the Pontine Region surveys from protohistory to the Roman period.

during the Roman period, we need to be able to link the ceramics related to the kilns with their actual distribution over the landscape.[20] This needs further classification of especially the common wares through archaeometric analysis, which is currently being undertaken as part of the PhD research of Filmo Verhagen, carried out at the University of Uppsala (Sweden) and Barbara Borgers at the University of Vienna (Austria).

Why an Integrated Database for the Suburbium of Rome?

While we plan further work on the Pontine Region database and to extend it with legacy data over the next years, at the same time we have started to work on the integration of the Pontine Region database with those created by the Suburbium project of Sapienza University and the Tiber Valley Project of the British School. This so-called Rome Hinterland Project (RHP) will facilitate the type of socio-economic and demographic analyses presented above on a wide scale for Rome's hinterland. Below, we first describe the relevance of the RHP initiative, followed by the challenges the RHP consortium encounters in realizing the objective of an integrated database for the Suburbium that is moreover expandable with other projects.

In debates on ancient demography and the nature of the ancient economy, ceramic data from archaeological surveys is increasingly used as an important source, as ceramics can attribute chronology, function and status to archaeological sites recorded in surveys.[21] As such, we can use survey data as proxies to reconstruct patterns of production, trade and consumption[22] and, to some extent, to approximate population levels and trends.[23] Ceramic analysis is a tool that, independently from historical sources, is instrumental in classifying archaeological sites within a chronological and functional spectrum of settlement forms. By combining classified site data, one can proceed to map settlement patterns on a regional scale.

The classification and dating of sites within a single survey is useful to reconstruct the settlement patterns on the scale of that survey and to relate these patterns to local urban centres, landscape and infrastructure. Yet, we need to aggregate datasets for macro-regional and interregional socio-economic and demographic analyses, as is the case with the Suburbium of Rome, for which multiple datasets exist. However, as we will explain below, aggregating datasets faces us with challenges and is time-consuming. Why take all this painstaking effort to integrate survey data and databases? One of the principal reasons is that aggregating survey databases from around Rome – where large tracts of land were, and still are, available for archaeological study – provides us with one of the few (if not only) opportunities to study the impact of the foundation, growth and decline of an ancient metropolis on its immediate hinterland. Substantively, the RHP team is convinced that bringing together site and pottery data for the hinterland of Rome will be a fundamental tool in the study of longer-term socio-economic trends quantitatively, qualitatively and comparatively. We are, for example, interested in:

- the diversity of land use and the rural settled landscape
- production and consumption patterns
- economic performance and standard of living
- rural demography
- intra-regional synchronic and diachronic comparison

Fig. 5 shows a comparison of settlement trends in sample areas in four landscapes in the Pontine plain from the Archaic period into the late Imperial period; it shows the potential of aggregate datasets to make comparisons between landscape zones. The Roman hinterland database would allow such analyses on a much wider scale, comprising the various landscape zones around Rome. Similarly, we may use the classification of rural sites to come to demographic inferences, as we discussed above using the example of *Antium* in the Pontine region.

To contextualize the integrated database of systematically collected rural survey data in the landscapes that make up the hinterland of Rome, we can make use of a large body of archaeological knowledge on cities, ports, towns, road and production infrastructure as well as on a range of rural site types (farmsteads, villas, hamlets, villages, production facilities) mapped in other projects than our own. Such information is gathered from the already mentioned Forma Italiae inventories, and from local site inventories and excavations. The incorporation of these data will be indispensable to use the aggregate quantitative data to carry out sophisticated spatial analyses of the economy and demography of Rome's hinterland. Cartographical data on the physical aspects of the landscape and past topography is incorporated in the consortium's separate GIS databases.

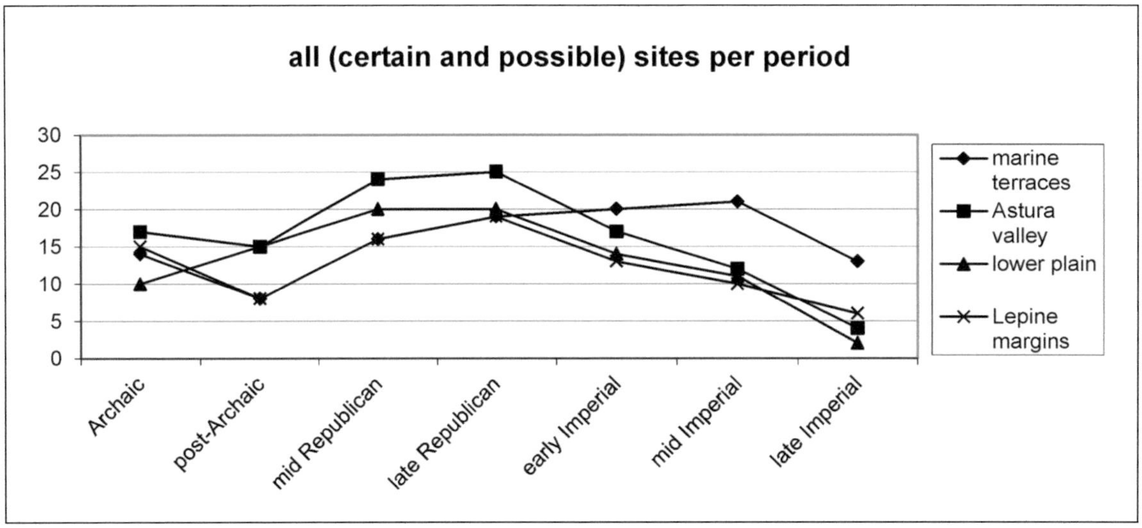

Fig. 5: Comparative approach of settlement dynamics between the Archaic and Imperial period in sample areas in four landscapes in the Pontine plain.

Challenges in Creating a Survey Database for the Pontine Region Project

Data integration is however not straightforward and requires several preparatory steps. A first step is updating and homogenizing the databases for each project individually. Below we illustrate this exercise for the Pontine Region Project database, by discussing how we have recently dealt with challenges in site- and pottery chronology and site classification.

Issues of Site-Chronology: Examples from Crustumerium and the Pontine Region

Concurrent with the excavations of the cemeteries and settlement of Crustumerium, the Groningen Institute of Archaeology has carried out resurveys of parts of the urban and rural areas of the ancient town.[24] Its aim was to increase our understanding of legacy survey datasets created in the 1970s within the framework of the Latium Vetus surveys[25] and in the 1990s, as part of the Suburbium project.[26] The pottery data collected in the 1970s were interpreted as proof that many sites were settled as early as the proto-historical period. However, the principal researcher, Jorn Seubers, found that the ceramic types on which the early chronology of find assemblages were foremost based (i.e. red fired coarse ware tile and pottery), of find assemblages in Crustumerium's urban context, were consistently consistently associated with *bucchero* and *impasto rosso* (i.e. late 7th/6th century BC). These findings lined up with insights made by colleagues from Sapienza University.[27] The same 7th/6th century BC wares were largely absent in rural sites containing similar coarse ware fabrics. Instead, black gloss (from the mid-4thcentury BC onwards), which was sporadic in the urban area, was the primary pottery class associated with (red firing) coarse wares in rural assemblages.[28] Comparing associations of coarse wares with the distribution of fine wares for the urban area of Crustumerium and the surrounding countryside thus demonstrated that there are significant differences between the two. This is visualized in figure 6: the upper histogram tabulates find contexts from the urban area showing a consistent Orientalising to Archaic dating pattern with substantial numbers of diagnostic *impasto rosso* and *bucchero* sherds thought to match the dates of the bulk of the finds. This would be congruent with the historically and archaeologically attested abandonment of the settlement of Crustumerium and its cemeteries around 500 BC. The lower histograms in fig. 6, however, which tabulate find contexts from the rural territory, show an abundance of black glazed ware, dating to the Republican period and only a few diagnostics for the Orientalising and Archaic periods. This suggests that there is a bias in the chronology provided for the bulk of the material reported from the countryside in the surveys of the 1970s. Considering the scarcity of diagnostic pottery evidence on sites attributed to the protohistoric periods (750–500 BC) many of these rural sites probably should be dated after the abandon-

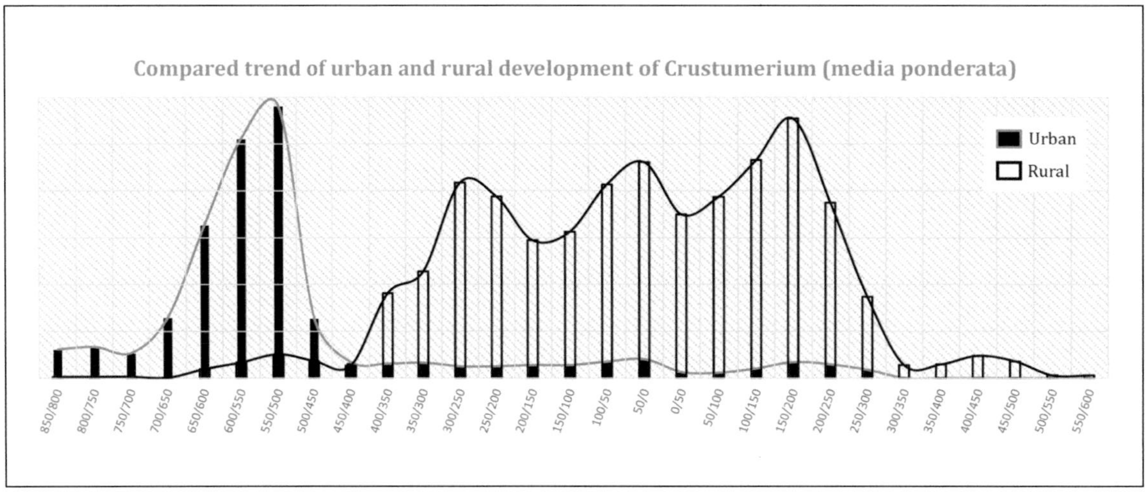

Fig. 6: The frequency of the occurrence of specific chronological intervals in the pottery collected in the urban survey and in the rural survey of the GIA. The compared pottery consumption trends clearly illustrate how different the urban and rural ceramic records are, and show how pottery consumption in the countryside starts to increase especially after the abandonment of Crustumerium.

ment of the settlement. The two maps in figures 7a, b illustrate the consequences. The upper map plots the 'legacy' scenario (i.e. providing consistently early dates for impasto and coarse wares); in the lower map, the sites have been filtered on the presence of diagnostic materials with 7th/6th century dates. When these are compared, the impact becomes clear regarding our understanding of the nature and intensity of ruralisation of Crustumerium. In this particular case there is a potential drop in sites from approximately 150 to 30. Although individual sites might hide earlier phases, the ruralisation around Crustumerium during the Archaic period was certainly less intense than previously postulated. The key to such critical reviews is the greater insight that pottery specialists have obtained since the 1980s in the actual date ranges of impasto and coarse wares. These ranges appeared to be much longer than protohistoric landscape archaeologists, including the authors, thought them to be. The above case shows the importance of acknowledging pottery dating issues, and the realization that this may lead to very different scenarios of urban and rural development. It also shows the need for transparency regarding analytical choices. Below we highlight another challenge when integrating survey data, attributing function to sites.

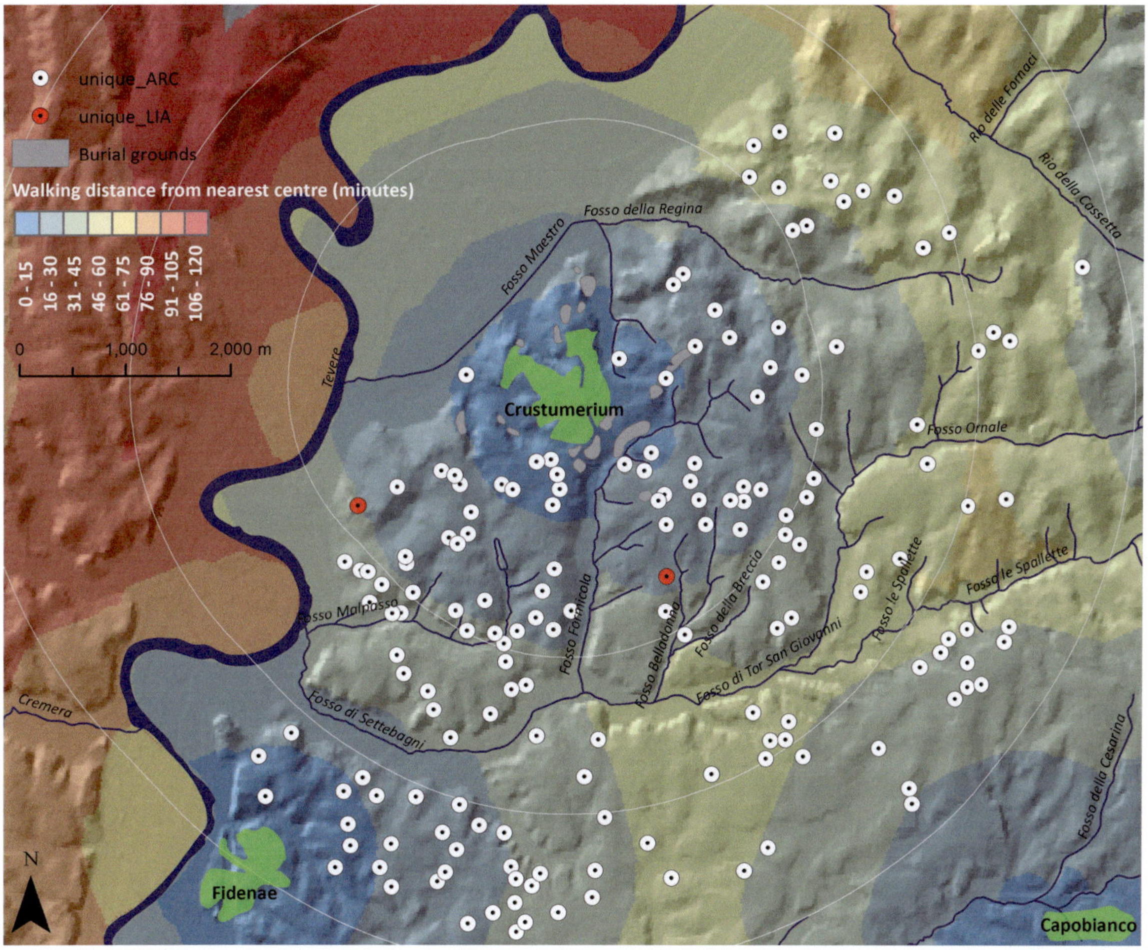

Fig. 7a: Recorded observations of surface ceramics of Orientalising/Archaic date, in a 5 km radius around Crustumerium based on Latium Vetus and Suburbium data.

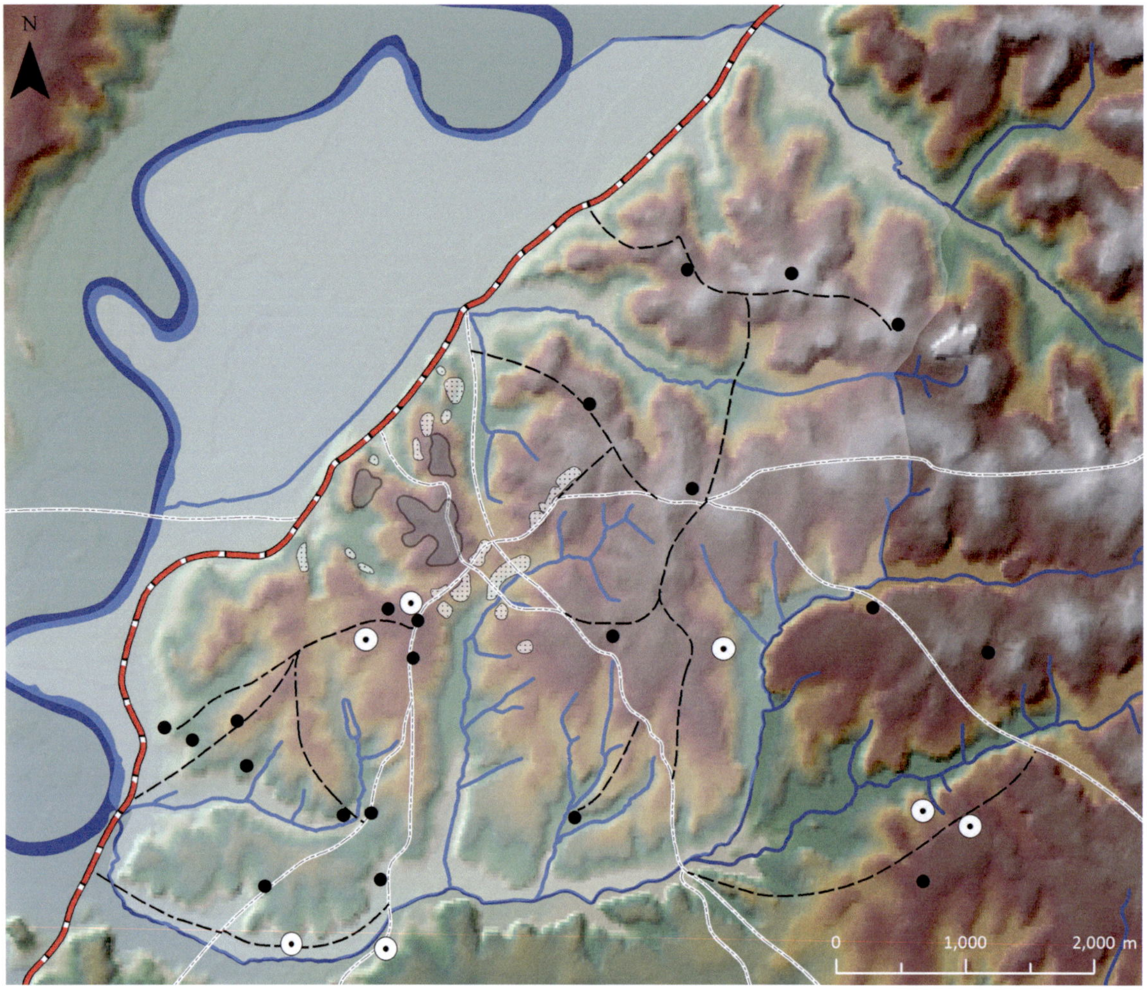

Fig. 7b: An overview of the urban and rural layout of Crustumerium according to the "low count" of Archaic evidence (transparent white = territory, grey = urban area, white dotted = funerary areas), marked with larger and smaller rural sites (white and black) and primary (white) and secondary roads (dashed).

Issues with Determining Site Function

Another challenge concerns the functional analysis of survey pottery from archaeological sites. What functions can we assign to the dots (sites) on our survey maps on the basis of surface finds? Are we dealing with a farmstead, a villa, a rural sanctuary, a tomb, or a kiln? In 2011, Carter and Prieto published part of the Metapontino survey in detail and showed how a functional analysis of assemblages of potsherds from regional survey can result in a classification of sites as tombs, farmhouses, and rural sanctuaries.[29] For the Pontine Region, we have used similar approaches.[30] Tol (2012), for instance, showed how intra-site analysis on the basis of hyper-intensive surveys may go further and reveal functional areas within sites, such as the pottery production part of a modest farmstead's economy, even if the relevant material is only a fraction (0.01%) of the total amount of material diagnosed.

There is no doubt that, if we want to use our site data quantitatively, we have to aggregate our data in functional classes. While self-evident, the compatibility between local site classifications based on the functional interpretation of assemblages is not a straightforward exercise even within one region, and will depend on a careful selection of attributes. Most scholars will agree that functional interpretations of artefact assemblages in combination with scatter size is the basis of site classification. However, when aiming to compare classified sites between individual surveys, we must be sure that we compare like with like. The difficulty here is that we need to group sites under a single site classification label that may have very different material manifestations in the landscape, depending on a range of cultural and landscape factors. Also, classifications are often rigid and do not easily accommodate multiple functions. To illustrate the problem: the material manifestation of a mid-Republican farmstead on the marine terraces in the Pontine Region is different from that of a mid-Republican farmstead on the slopes of the Monti Lepini; while the first consists of a scatter of pottery and building materials, the second may have a platform of drystone masonry of polygonal blocks on which the farmhouse was built. Do the different material manifestations mean that both site types nonetheless belong to the same class of medium sized isolated farmsteads, or do the platform sites perhaps represent a separate class of farms, more geared at the market-oriented production of olive-oil?[31] Another example: for the Roman period it is very difficult to distinguish between funerary contexts, farmsteads, and (some) votive deposits. These largely contain the same wares, especially when deposits contain largely pottery shapes and no figurines, such as at Casarinaccio in Ardea and votive deposit II in Satricum.[32]

Challenges in Creating a Survey Database for the Roman Suburbium

With individual databases updated and standardized, the next challenge in integrating different project databases was solving issues of compatibility between the different projects involved within the RHP. Individual survey projects use different ceramic and site classification schemes based on different criteria that are often not made explicit. Between projects, pottery classifications will have different breakdowns of chronological periods and different chronological ranges attributed to ceramic wares, while different terminologies will be used. Site classifications will be based on varying criteria.[33] When aiming at aggregate, macro-regional and comparative analyses, the issue then becomes how to make ceramic and site data from multiple projects and case studies compatible for quantitative diachronic analyses. This is fundamental if we want to do the various types of analyses that we have referred to above for the Pontine Region on an even larger scale.

Hence, the challenges faced by the consortium of the Pontine Region Project, the Suburbium Project, and the Tiber Valley Project prior to the migration of their pottery and site classification data into the shared RHP database can be summed up under three headings:

1. reaching consensus on the semantic level. This means agreeing on similar ways of classifying pottery as to wares and shapes, and similar ways of classifying sites
2. reaching consensus on pottery chronologies to facilitate dating of sites
3. finding solutions to the technical challenge of bringing together separate databases within one overarching database structure.

These aims were addressed by the RHP consortium in various workshops in Groningen, in Rome (at the British School and at Sapienza University), in Durham, and in Cologne between 2015 and 2018. In the 2015 Rome workshop, for instance, pottery specialists of the three projects brought 'problematic' pottery categories to the workshop and discussed them, such as the supposedly Archaic coarse wares (to which we referred above in a case study concerning the site of Crustumerium). The outcome was positive: the group encountered no major obstacles to devise a classification into which pottery from all three projects could fit. It appeared that standard procedures for site classification and dating were shared by all three groups. Moreover, it was found that no major differences appeared in terms of the presence/absence of pottery wares and that the three projects broadly used the same ceramic typologies and chronologies. The group noted, however, differences on the level of database structure, and had to work on a common vocabulary for pottery classes and chronologies for non-local pottery wares and shapes.

Conclusions

In this paper we have given an update of the status quo of the Pontine Region database and given examples of analyses that we have carried out so far, showing its potential for studying the Pontine economy and demography on the level of the whole region, as well as comparatively between its constituent local rural landscapes and towns. We have also highlighted the potential of incorporating legacy data in the Pontine Region database, which would significantly broaden the quantitative basis with which to perform analyses. At the same time, we have commented on the challenges this poses to integrating data recorded in older topographic surveys with those obtained in modern systematic surveys. Next, we discussed the initiative of merging the Tiber Valley Project database, the Suburbium database, and the Pontine Region Project database in one overarching Rome Hinterland database. This initiative will result in one of the largest databases of its kind, holding many thousands of site and pottery records for the hinterland of Rome. For the first time, the RHP database will allow for detailed diachronic socio-economic and demographic analyses of the hinterland of an ancient metropolis over a timespan of more than ten centuries. Having taken the steps of data preparation and consensus building regarding typologies, chronologies and terminologies, the international RHP consortium is in the crucial phase of preparing for data-migration and finalizing the overarching database structure. Once the basic design of the database has been established, the group will plan the first analyses of the pottery and site records, write a technical publication and a position paper. At the same time, however, we are looking forward to extending the project to include other datasets, projects and scholars. The aim is to expand the project in the form of an 'open' structure that will benefit the larger archaeological community. We believe that concerted efforts to bring together regional pottery and site datasets in overarching databases is the way for survey archaeology to move forward if we want to answer detailed questions of demographic, socio-economic and cultural developments on a larger scale.

Notes

[1] De Haas et al. 2011.

[2] See Tol 2017.

[3] Attema 2018.

[4] Morley 1996; Witcher 2005.

[5] The project 'Integrating Archaeological Field Surveys – Rome and Beyond' (project number 236-61-002) is funded by NWO for a period of four years between 2016–2020. The consortium also received financial support from the British Academy, for which it is likewise very grateful.

[6] cf. De Haas – Tol forthcoming.

[7] Van Leusen et al. 2010.

[8] Lugli 1926, 1928.

[9] Brandizzi Vittucci 1977.

[10] Piccarreta 1977.

[11] cf. Witcher 2008.

[12] Attema et al. 2008; 2010 and 2011; Tol 2012.

[13] Piccarreta 1977.

[14] Attema et al. 2011.

[15] Tol 2017; Attema – De Haas 2011.

[16] cf. De Haas et al. 2011.

[17] Tol 2017.

[18] Attema – De Haas 2011.

[19] Tol et al. 2014; Tol – Borgers 2016.

[20] Borgers et al. 2018a and b.

[21] e.g. Launaro 2011.

[22] Millett 2000.

[23] Sbonias 1999; Drennan et al. 2012.

[24] Attema et al. 2014.

[25] Quilici – Quilici Gigli 1980.
[26] Carafa – Capanna 2007.
[27] Carafa – Capanna 2009.
[28] Seubers – Tol 2016, figs. 10. 11.
[29] Keith Swift in Carter – Prieto 2011, 129–142.
[30] De Haas 2011; Attema et al. 2013/2014.
[31] De Haas et al. 2012.
[32] di Mario, 2005; Bouma 1996.
[33] Fulminante 2014, 131–141.

Image Credits

Fig. 1: map T. de Haas, after de Haas – Tol forthcoming fig. 1. – Fig. 2: map T. de Haas, after Attema – de Haas 2011, fig. 5.10. – Fig. 3a: after de Haas 2011, fig. 7. – Fig. 3b: after de Haas 2011, fig. 8. – Fig. 4: map T. de Haas. – Fig. 5: de Haas 2011, fig. 6.9. – Fig. 6: Seubers – Tol 2016, fig. 14. – Fig. 7a: Seubers 2018, fig. 5.36A. – Fig. 7b: Seubers 2018, fig. 5.46.

References

Attema 2018
P. A. J. Attema, Urban and Rural Landscapes of the Pontine Region (Central Italy) in the Late Republican Period, Economic Growth between Colonial Heritage and Elite Impetus, BABesch 93, 2018, 143–164.

Attema – De Haas 2011
P. A. J. Attema – T. C. A. de Haas, Rural Settlement and Population Extrapolation, a Case Study from the Ager of Antium, Central Italy (350 BC – AD 400), in: A. Bowman – A. Wilson (eds.), Settlement, Urbanisation and Population. Oxford Studies on the Roman Economy, 2011, vol. 2 (Oxford 2011) 97–140.

Attema et al. 2008
P. A. J. Attema – H. Feiken – T. C. A. De Haas – G. W. Tol – M. La Rosa, The Astura and Nettuno surveys of the Pontine Region Project (2003–2005): 1st interim report, Palaeohistoria, 2008, 49/50, 415–516.

Attema et al. 2010
P. A. J. Attema – T. C. A. de Haas – G. W. Tol, The Astura and Nettuno Surveys of the Pontine Region Project (2003–2005), 2nd and Final Report, Palaeohistoria 51/52, 2010, 169–327.

Attema et al. 2011
P. A. J. Attema – T. C. A. De Haas – G. W. Tol, Between Satricum and Antium. Settlement Dynamics in a Coastal Landscape in Latium Vetus (Leuven 2011).

Attema et al. 2013/2014
P. A. J. Attema – T. C. A. de Haas – G. W. Tol, Villas and Farmsteads in the Ager Setinus (Sezze, Italy), Palaeohistoria 55/56, 2013/2014, 177–244.

Attema et al. 2014
P. A. J. Attema – F. di Gennaro – J. F. Seubers – B. Belelli-Marchesini – B. Ullrich, Early Urbanization at Crustumerium (9th and 5th B.C.), in: E. Robinson (ed.), Current Approaches to the Archaeology of First Millennium BC Italian Urbanism, JRA Suppl. 97, 2014, 175–196.

Attema et al. 2017
P. A. J. Attema – T. C. A. de Haas – J. F. Seubers – G. W. Tol, In Search of the Archaic Countryside. Different Scenarios for the Ruralisation of *Satricum* and *Crustumerium,* in: P. Lulof – C. Smith (eds.), The Age of Tarquinius. Central Italy in the Late 6th Century (Leuven 2017) 195–204.

Borgers et al. 2018a
B. Borgers – G. W. Tol – T. C. A. de Haas, Reconstructing Production Technology and Distribution, Using thin Section Petrography: A Pilot Study of Roman Pottery Production in the Pontine Region, Central Italy, JASc Reports 21, 1064–1072.

Borgers et al. 2018b
B. Borgers – G. W. Tol – T. C. A. de Haas, Roman Cooking Vessels (ollae): a Preliminary Study of the Material from the Pontine Region, Central Italy, STAR: Science & Technology of Archaeological Research, DOI: 10.1080/20548923.2018.1445824.

Brandizzi Vittucci 1968
P. Brandizzi Vittucci, Cora (Rome 1968).

Bouma 1996
J. W. Bouma, Religio Votiva: The Archaeology of Latial Votive Religion (PhD thesis Groningen 1996).

Carafa – Capanna 2009
P. Carafa – M. C. Capanna, Il Progetto 'Archeologia del Suburbio di Roma' per la ricostruzione dei paesaggi agrari antichi, in: V. Jolivet – C. Pavolini – M. A. Tomei – R. Volpe (eds.), Suburbium 2, Collection de L'École Francaise de Rome 419, 2009, 27–39.

Carter – Prieto 2011
J. C. Carter – A. Prieto (eds.), The Chora of Metaponto 3, Archaeological Field Survey, Bradano to Basento, University of Texas Press (Austin 2011).

De Haas 2011
T. C. A. de Haas, Fields, Farms and Colonists. Intensive Field Survey and Early Roman Colonization in the Pontine Region, Central Italy (Groningen 2011).

De Haas et al. 2011
T. C. A. de Haas – G. W. Tol – P. A. J. Attema, Investing in the Colonia and Ager of Antium, Facta 5, 2011, 111–144.

De Haas et al. 2012
T. C. A. de Haas – P. A. J. Attema – G. W. Tol, Platform Sites along the Lepine Mountains: A Review of the Data Gathered by the Pontine Region Project, Palaeohistoria 53/54, 2012, 195–282.

De Haas – Tol forthcoming
T. C. A. de Haas – G. W. Tol, The Analytical Potential of Intensive Field Survey Data: Developments in the Collection, Analysis and Interpretation of Surface Ceramics within the Pontine Region Project, in: A. Meens – M. Nazou – W. van de Put (eds.), Fields, Sherds and Scholars. Recording and Interpreting Survey Ceramics (forthcoming).

Di Mario 2005
F. Di Mario, Ardea, il deposito votivo di Casarinaccio (Rome 2005).

Drennan et al. 2015
R. Drennan – A. Berrey – C. Peterson, Regional Settlement Demography in Archaeology (New York 2015).

Fulminante 2014
F. Fulminante, The Urbanization of Rome and Latium Vetus: from the Bronze Age to the Archaic Era (Cambridge 2014).

Launaro 2011
A. Launaro, Peasants and Slaves: The Rural Population of Roman Italy (200 BC to AD 100) (Cambridge 2011).

Lugli 1926
G. Lugli, Anxur-Tarracina (Rome 1926).

Lugli 1928
G. Lugli, Circeii (Rome 1928).

Millet 2000
M. Millett, Dating, Quantifying and Utilizing Pottery Assemblages from Surface Survey, in: R. Francovich – H. Patterson (eds), Extracting Meaning from Ploughsoil Assemblages (Oxford 2000) 53–59.

Morley 1996
N. Morley, Metropolis and Hinterland: The City of Rome and the Italian Economy, 200 BC–AD 200 (Cambridge 1996).

Picarreta 1977
F. Piccarreta, Astura (Firenze 1977).

Sbonias 1999
K. Sbonias, Introduction to Issues in Demography and Survey, in: J. Bintliff – K. Sbonias (eds.), Reconstructing Past Population Trends in Mediterranean Europe (Oxford 1999) 1–20.

Seubers 2018,
J. F. Seubers, Scratching through the Surface, Revisiting the Archaeology of City and Country in Crustumerium and North Latium Vetus between 850 and 300 BC (PhD. diss. Groningen 2018).

Seubers – Tol 2016
J. F. Seubers – G. W. Tol, City, Country and Crisis in the Ager Crustuminus, Confronting Legacy Data with Resurvey Results in the Territory of Ancient Crustumerium, Palaeohistoria 57/58, 2016, 137–234.

Tol 2012

G. W. Tol, A Fragmented History. A Methodological and Artefactual Approach to the Study of Ancient Settlement in the Territories of Satricum and Antium (Groningen 2012).

Tol 2017

G. W. Tol, From Surface find to Consumption Trend: a Ceramic Perspective on the Economic History of the Pontine Region (Lazio, Central Italy) in the Roman Period, in: T. C. A. de Haas – G. W. Tol (eds.), The Economic Integration of Roman Italy. Rural Communities in a Globalizing World (Leiden 2017) 367–387.

Tol et al. 2014

G. W. Tol – T. C. A. de Haas – K. Armstrong – P. A. J. Attema, Minor Centres in the Pontine Plain: the Cases of Forum Appii and Ad Medias, BSR 82, 2014, 109–134.

Tol – Borgers 2016

G. W. Tol – B. Borgers, An Integrated Approach to the Study of Local Production and Exchange in the lower Pontine Plain, JRA 29, 2016, 349–370.

Van Leusen et al. 2010

P. M. van Leusen – G. W. Tol – C. Anastasia, Archaeological Sites Recorded by the GIA Hidden Landscapes Survey Campaigns in the Monti Lepini (Lazio, Italy), 2005–2009, Palaeohistoria 51/52, 2010, 329–424.

Witcher 2005

R. Witcher, The Extended Metropolis: Urbs, Suburbium and Population, JRA 18, 2005, 120–138.

Witcher 2008

R. Witcher, (Re)Surveying Mediterranean Rural Landscapes: GIS and Legacy Survey Data, Internet Archaeology 24, 2008 (https://doi.org/10.11141/ia.24.2).

A View from the Margins: Interamna Lirenas and its Territory in the Long Term[1]

Alessandro Launaro

The Roman conquest of the Mediterranean created a unified political space, which brought about unprecedented conditions that favoured trade and exchange across the whole expanse of the ancient Mediterranean and beyond. It is impossible to deny the relevance and impressive scale of Mediterranean exchange and integration at the peak of the Roman Empire. But it is quite a different thing to assume that because of such remarkable levels of integration everything managed to get everywhere and in comparably high volumes. Such assumptions tend to over-emphasise the impact of overseas trade at the expense of (comparably less-understood) local production, distribution and consumption patterns. As a result, our understanding of landscapes located at the margins of the Mediterranean trade network could in fact be seriously affected by their reduced archaeological visibility. These problems can be properly framed and evaluated by exploring distribution and consumption patterns in an area that appears to have been only marginally affected by the input of overseas trade. Notwithstanding this, it does not appear to have declined, at least not for a while and not so dramatically.

Since 2010 the Roman town of Interamna Lirenas and its immediate hinterland, in the Liri Valley (Southern Lazio, Italy), have been the subject of an integrated research project run by the Faculty of Classics of the University of Cambridge, under the direction of Martin Millett and myself, in partnership with the Italian Soprintendenza (G. R. Bellini, SABAP-Lazio) and the Municipality of Pignataro Interamna (Bellini et al. 2014). Throughout history, the Valley has represented a natural inland corridor between Lazio and Campania, and Interamna appears to have been well-placed to play a part in the movement of people and goods across the region and far beyond it, through the Liri-Garigliano river and the port of Minturnae (Launaro 2019). One way to map the place of Interamna within these networks and also the relationship between the town and its territory is to look at the relative proportions of specific classes of material culture as they developed over time. In order to achieve that, two separate-but-related pottery datasets will be discussed: one derived from four seasons of intensive field survey across the countryside (2010–13), the other from the first two seasons of excavation of the theatre (2013–14).

If we consider the chronological distribution of finds, both town and countryside seem to have followed broadly similar trends. However, if we compare the absolute amount of imports to the total amount of finds across the period, it becomes obvious that they only represented a tiny fraction of the material culture consumed in both town and countryside. It is local/regional commonwares that represent the absolute majority of finds in both datasets and do in fact provide a far more comprehensive and reliable picture of the development of production, distribution and consumption patterns in the area.

As a result, we find ourselves in the position to contrast and compare two views of the same landscape: a) one including commonwares, b) the other based only on the recovery of finewares and main amphorae types. For decades, the latter view has been the basis on which the practice of landscape archaeology in Italy appears to have rested. The resulting long-term settlement patterns would lend themselves to strikingly different interpretations: a) significant early growth and stability well into the 3rd century AD followed by decline, as opposed to b) limited growth followed by an early decline already by the end of the 1st century BC.

The fact that relative volumes of comparable material culture evolved in a similar way in both town and countryside supports the idea that town and countryside were mutually dependent and shared broadly similar patterns of material culture. However, the underlying distribution and consumption patterns were rooted in local/regional networks, whose existence and performance was largely independent of that Mediterranean-wide exchange and integration so visibly promoted by the Roman empire.

Notes

[1] This text provides an extended abstract of a study, which has since been published elsewhere: Launaro – Leone 2018.

References

Bellini et al. 2014

G. R. Bellini – A. Launaro – M. Millett, Roman Colonial Landscapes: Interamna Lirenas and Its Territory through Antiquity, in: J. Pelgrom – T. Stek (eds.), Roman Republican Colonisation: New Perspectives from Archaeology and Ancient History (Rome 2014) 255–275.

Launaro 2019

A. Launaro, Interamna Lirenas – a History of 'Success'? Long-term Trajectories across Town and Countryside (4th c. BC to 5th c. AD), in: A. U. De Giorgi (eds.), Cosa and the Colonial Landscape of Republican Italy (Third and Second Century BC) (Ann Arbor 2019) 119–138.

Launaro – Leone 2018

A. Launaro – N. Leone, A View from the Margin? Roman Commonwares and Patterns of Distribution and Consumption at Interamna Lirenas (Lazio), JRA 31, 2018, 323–338.

Production and Trade in Late Republican and Imperial Inland Etruria: Integrating Archaeological and Archaeometric Results of the Val di Pesa and Val Orme-Project

Günther Schörner – Veronika Schreck

The Vienna Orme and Pesa valley Project (VOPP) studies a micro-region defined by the two river valleys of Orme and Pesa between the surroundings of Empoli in the Arno plain and the more mountainous territory to the south of Northern inland Tuscany.[1] The general aim of the project is to investigate changes and continuities in different aspects of human behaviour in the landscape, with a special focus on problems of site definition and site classification (e.g. villas and villa landscapes), as well as the relationship between town and country. The starting point of the research was Molino San Vincenzo, which has been studied by a large array of different methodologies.[2] Geophysical prospections helped to identify a large rural building but the excavation revealed that the ancient building was heavily damaged by modern agricultural activities.[3]

In order to characterise the site of Molino San Vincenzo by its material culture and to better define urban-rural-relations in northern Roman Etruria, it was necessary to compare the pottery assemblage of Molino San Vincenzo with pottery from the neighbouring Roman town, modern Empoli.[4] These studies also helped to understand the trade connections and the flow of goods in the study area and in Northern Etruria.[5]

The urban site of Pratesi was excavated from 1980 till 1982.[6] It is situated in the medieval city centre of Empoli, which is in the location of the Roman town. The findings come from a filling of two big supply containers of uncertain dating. Most of the pottery found is to be dated in Roman times, but the material was heavily mixed and it was not possible to identify any stratigraphic sequence. Because of the large amount of the sherds, the entire assemblage can be characterised as secondary refuse representative for the pottery used in the town over a long period and from different contexts.

To establish a typology of the sherds found at both sites, archaeometrical analyses have been undertaken. C. Capelli from the University of Genova analysed and classified 60 samples via thin section. With the help of this data, it was possible to catalogue most of the findings and to categorize the pottery found as local, regional or supraregional products.[7] Referring to antique sources, the term *local* is defined as the distance which could be walked there and back in the same day. Under consideration of slope and travel speed, cost-distance can be calculated using Empoli and Molino San Vincenzo as starting points and categorizing distances in different colours (fig. 1).[8]

The most important group of the pottery under investigation is fabric A, a locally produced sherd type.[9] Numerous forms like beakers, jugs, pots, bowls, plates, and amphorae of different date were made in this fabric. The typical temper of these fabrics is

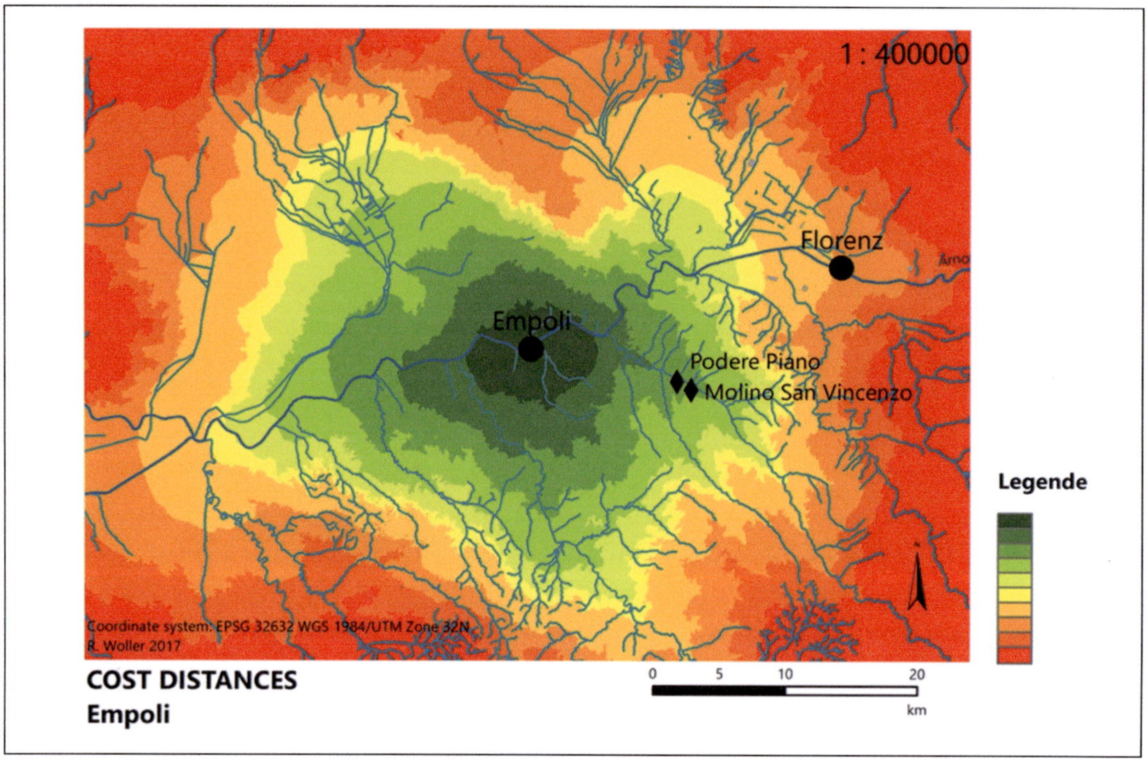

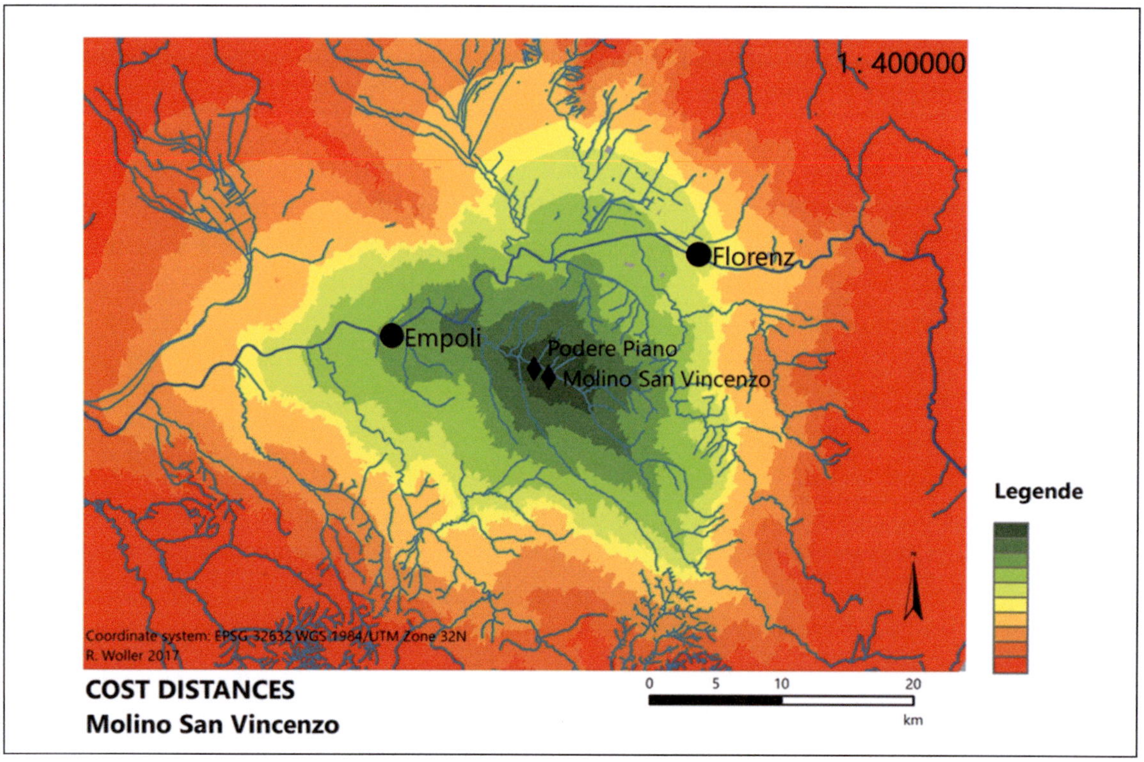

Fig. 1: Coast Distance Maps: Empoli and Molino San Vincenzo

microfossils like *foraminifera* and *radiolaria.* Clay deposits are located near the modern town of Empoli, for example on the right bank of the river Arno.

The largest group of coarse wares belongs to fabric C. It was produced with raw material, which originates from the region of Montaione or the Monti Pisani. Therefore, vessels of this fabric were imported regionally from the Elsa Valley or from the Pisa region.[10] Another regional fabric may also have been produced in the area of Pisa, although further deposits of such temper material are attested elsewhere. This fabric E is tempered with calcite particles, which are discernible due to their angular and mostly transparent to light opaque grains. It was exclusively used for cooking ware as the calcite particles have an excellent heat coefficient. Fabric D was also primarily used for cooking wares. Aside from quartz and feldspar, the temper typically consists of mafic minerals. One outcrop of these minerals is located in the area of S. Casciano in Val di Pesa, and other occurrences are farther afield. Following the assumption that short transportation routes were preferred, fabric D is claimed also to be of local origin.

The comparison of the pottery found in Empoli, at the sites of Pratesi and Molino San Vincenzo revealed some peculiarities (fig. 2). One interesting phenomenon has been noted by comparing the cooking wares of both sites. A large part of the cooking ware from Empoli was made of fabric E and other fabrics, which can be traced to Campania and North Africa and which were imported supra-regionally to Empoli; pottery made of fabric E and especially imports from further away are attested at Molino San Vincenzo to a much lesser extent. In contrast, the local fabric D is strongly attested both at Empoli and Molino San Vincenzo. Also, the regional fabric C was found in large amounts especially at Molino San Vincenzo. Regarding Empoli, the distribution of fabrics can easily be explained with its infrastructural connection. Due to its location along the main west-east connection routes, the *via Quincita* and the Arno river, regionally fabricated

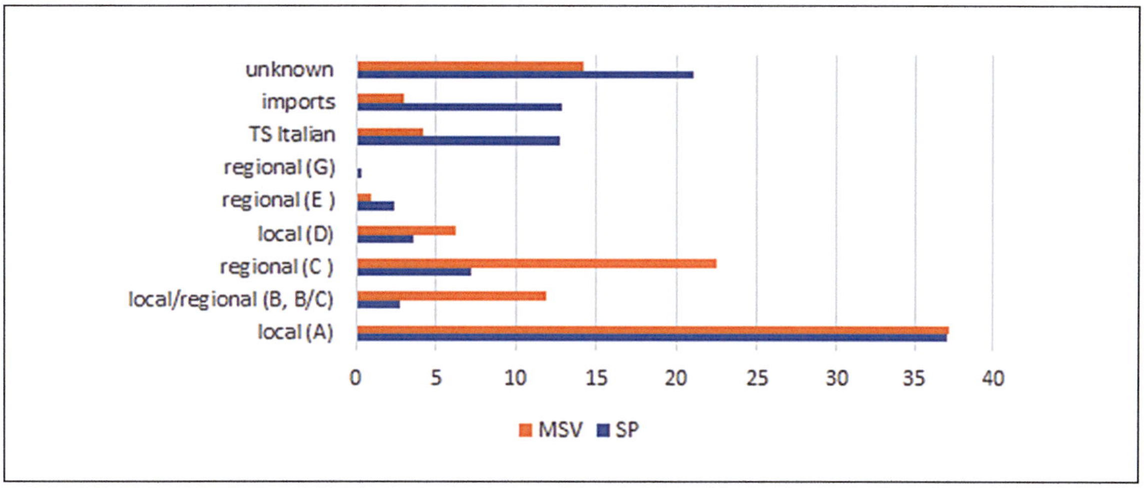

Fig. 2: Fabrics of the Urban Centre (SP) and its Hinterland (MSV)

vessels and supra-regionally imports were easily available. Thus, Empoli was a consumer itself but probably also played the role of distribution centre for its hinterland.

The distribution pattern of cooking ware fabrics of Molino San Vincenzo is more difficult to explain. It leads to the question as to why the regional fabric C is overrepresented compared to the local fabric D, since it was produced in a more remote area. It indicates close ties to the Pisa region. Supraregional imports of cooking ware like internal red slip vessels or African cooking ware, however, are lacking in the rural context. This leads to the interpretation that the purchasing of pottery in Molino San Vincenzo concentrated on the local and most accessible regional market, as these fabrics dominate. The cooking ware of Empoli however, shows an excellent integration in the local, regional, and supraregional trade networks. This pattern follows the overall trend of the entire pottery findings of both sites. Aside from the locally produced fabric A, which is represented very well in both cases, a trend towards vessels of local and regional fabrics can be observed in the hinterland. Generally, the acquisition of goods in Molino San Vincenzo seems to concentrate on the local micro-level and the nearest and easiest accessible regional level; while in Empoli, a vital exchange of goods is recognizable via imports of regional goods but also of supraregional amphorae, table ware and cooking ware. Empoli may have been the distribution centre for Molino San Vincenzo although, for example, vessels of fabric C are numerous at Molino San Vincenzo but not well attested in the record of Empoli.

To conclude, thanks to the analysis of the fabrics found in Empoli and its hinterland a vital local and regional network of pottery production could be identified. Due to the research presented it was possible to identify Empoli as an important consumer city, but also as a distribution centre for the region of the middle Arno-valley for incoming and outgoing goods. The imported goods were probably transported from the Tyrrhenian coast upstream along the river Arno using the *via Quinctia* or the river itself. A stronger focus on the micro-level and regional level trade was identified for Molino San Vincenzo instead. The results of the research presented here correlate with survey results conducted in the *ager Pisanus* and *ager Volteranus.* Although farmsteads participated in exchange, the import of goods played a minor role and is mainly limited to easy accessible regional sources, while the urban centres were integrated in an empire-wide trade network.[11]

Notes

[1] Schörner 2020.

[2] Alderighi et al. 2011; Schörner – Terreni 2011; Schörner et al. 2013; Schörner et al. 2015; Hagmann – Schreck 2018.

[3] Schörner et al. 2013.

[4] Maiuri 2006.

[5] In general for trade in Northern Etruria: Menchelli – Pasquinucci 2006; Cantini 2010.
[6] Ferretti et al. 1995, fig. 21; Maiuri 2006, 29.
[7] Laurence 1999, 81 f.
[8] Schreck 2018, 17s. (based on Woller 2017).
[9] The following is a summary of Schreck 2018.
[10] In general to production sites of pottery in Northern Etruria: Olcese 2011, 27–45. 77–86.
[11] e.g. Pasquinucci et al. 2003.

Image Credits

All images by the authors.

References

Alderighi et al. 2011
L. Alderighi – G. Schörner – L. Terreni, Montespertoli (FI). Loc. Molino San Vincenzo: Campagna di scavo 2011, Notiziario della Soprintendenza per i Beni Archeologici della Toscana 7, 2011, 245–247.

Cantini 2010
F. Cantini, Circolazione, produzione e consumo di vasellame ceramico e anfore nel Medio Valdarno tra IV e VII Secolo: Nuovi dati da San Genesio (San Miniato, Pisa) e Firenze, in: S. Menchelli – S. S. Santoro – M. Pasquinucci – G. Guiducci (eds.), LRCW 3. Late Roman Coarse Wares, Cooking Wares and Amphorae in the Mediterranean Archaeology and Archaeometry Comparison between Western and Eastern Mediterranean, BARIntSer 2185, 2, 2010, 353–362.

Ferretti et al. 1995
E. Ferretti – R. Macii – L. Terreni (eds.), Ritrovamenti archeologici nel Territorio di Empoli (Florence 1995).

Hagmann – Schreck 2018
D. Hagmann – V. Schreck, Neue Forschungen zum ländlichen Fundplatz Molino San Vincenzo (Toskana, Italien), Akten des 16. Österreichischen Archäologentages am Institut für Klassische Archäologie Wien vom 25. bis 27. Februar 2016 (Vienna 2018) 163–174.

Laurence 1999
R. Laurence, The Roads of Roman Italy: Mobility and Cultural Change (London 1999).

Maiuri 2006
W. Maiuri, La Città, il Territorio, il Porto: Empoli in Età Romana, Milliarium 6 (Florence 2006) 28–39.

Menchelli – Pasquinucci 2006
S. Menchelli – M. Pasquinucci (eds.), Territorio e produzioni ceramiche. Paesaggi, economia e società in età romana, Atti del convegno internazionale Pisa 20–22 ottobre 2005 = Instrumenta 2 (2006).

Olcese 2011

G. Olcese, Atlante dei siti di produzione ceramica (Toscana, Lazio, Campania e Sicilia) con le tabelle dei principali relitti del mediterraneo occidentale con carichi dall'Italia centro meridionale. IV secolo a.C.–I secolo d.C., Immensa Aequora 2 (Rome 2012).

Pasquinucci et al. 2003

M. Pasquinucci – S. Menchelli – A. Del Rio, Archeologia a Vada Volaterrana: Il porto, i relitti, i commerci alla luce delle recenti acquisizioni, in: A. Benini – M. Giacobelli (eds.), Atti del II Convegno Nazionale di Archeologia Subacquea, Castiglioncello, 7–9 settembre 2001 (Santo Spirito 2003) 35–43.

Schörner – Terreni 2012

G. Schörner – L. Terreni, Montespertoli (FI). Loc. Molino San Vincenzo: Campagna di scavo 2012, Notiziario della Soprintendenza per i Beni Archeologici della Toscana 8, 2012, 332–334.

Schörner et al. 2013

G. Schörner – S. Groh – D. Hagmann – V. Schreck – L. Terreni, Montespertoli (FI). Loc. Molino San Vincenzo: Campagna di scavo 2013, Notiziario della Soprintendenza per i Beni Archeologici della Toscana 9, 2013, 310–314.

Schörner et al. 2015

G. Schörner – D. Hagmann – V. Schreck – L. G. Terreni, Montespertoli (FI). Molino San Vincenzo. Campagna di scavo agosto 2015 (concessione di scavo), Notiziario della Sopraintendenza per i Beni Archeologici della Toscana 11, 2015, 147–149.

Schörner 2020

G. Schörner (ed.), The Vienna orme and Pesa Valley Project. Proceedings of the International Workshop hald at Vienna, June 22–23, 2018, Roman Rural Landscapes Monograph Series vol. 1 (Vienna 2020).

Schreck 2018

V. Schreck, Die wirtschaftlichen Interaktionen im mittleren Arno-Tal am Beispiel der Keramik aus dem urbanen Zentrum von Empoli und den Siedlungen im Hinterland (PhD. Diss. Vienna 2018).

Woller 2017

R. Woller, Agricultural Modelling – Rekonstruktionsansätze zur römischen Landwirtschaft im Pesa-, Virginio-, Orme- und unteren Elsatal anhand von quantitativen Methoden (MA. Thesis University Vienna 2017).

The Archaeobotanical Study of Agriculture of Roman Peasants: Skilled Farmers of the 1st BC–5th AD in Tuscany, Central Italy

Anna Maria Mercuri – Eleonora Rattighieri – Rossella Rinaldi – Assunta Florenzano

Introduction

This paper focuses on the archaeobotanical study of small farmhouses and rural facilities on Roman sites in central Italy studied in the framework of the Roman Peasant Project. These rural sites were probably occupied during seasonal agricultural activities. The integrated analyses of pollen, non-pollen palynomorphs, charcoal particles, charcoal macroremains and seeds/fruits allowed us to obtain information on site function, associated land use, and the palaeoenvironment of these archaeological contexts. The landscape we deal with was open, sparsely wooded, and mainly consisted of pasture, and cereal and legume fields. Past economies were largely based on cultivation, animal breeding, and wood exploitation that induced changes in the plant cover by reducing trees and favouring crops and pasture plants. As agriculture basically consists of plant management and the control of fruit production and plant cycles, botanists are indispensable for the study of the actual functioning of the rural economies of the past. Such studies are preferably done in close cooperation with archaeologists working on the rural landscape. Moreover, the study of plant remains from archaeological layers is extremely useful when aiming at diachronic reconstructions of environmental changes, including the transformation of land use at the local scale.[1] Pollen and plant remains preserved from archaeological sites are the direct evidence of plants that lived as part of Nature or were manipulated as objects of Culture in the past.

In 2010, we started a botanical research on archaeological sites of central Italy within a multi-disciplinary archaeological project, the Roman Peasant Project, that focused on lower-class rural dwellers of southern Tuscany, under the direction of K. Bowes.[2] The Roman Peasant Project was begun in 2009 as a systematic investigation of Roman non-élites in the municipality of Cinigiano (Grosseto, southern Tuscany). The project started from the results of a surface survey carried out by M. Ghisleni during her PhD research, alongside the excavation of a cross-section of the smallest/poorest of these sites; the goal was to illuminate the complexity of Roman peasant life-ways and environmental interactions.[3] Then, it developed into an interdisciplinary project aiming to produce descriptions of the landscape and agrarian activity, and above all, to evaluate the diversity of what it meant to be “poor” in antiquity. Small farmhouses and rural facilities were studied in order to contribute to the understanding of agricultural development during Roman times.[4] Our archaeobotanical studies focused on environmental variables and habitat diversity of seven sites: Case Nuove, Colle Massari, Podere Marzuolo, Podere Terrato, Poggio dell'Amore, and San Martino, Tombarelle.

Methods

The investigated archaeological contexts lie upon gentle slopes in a rolling landscape of Mio-Pliocene clays which is dissected down to the level of the intermediate terrace of the Orcia-Ombrone river system. These constitute small rural sites, probably only occupied for seasonal activities during the 1st century BC to the 5th century AD. The sites represent a whole range of functions (e.g. temporary work area or barn, drain, agro-processing point, permanent habitation) that show a great human control over the surrounding productive landscape that required investment of labour and materials. Labour investment appears to be highly concentrated in time, especially from the end of the 1st century BC to the mid-1st century AD. Plant remains (pollen, non-pollen palynomorphs, charcoal particles, and seeds and fruits) revealed functions of the sites as well as the environmental conditions for living and producing in this landscape.[5]

We studied 87 pollen samples and 84 samples containing macroremains. These were taken from a variety of contexts together representing a cross-section of the size and typology of the archaeological sites recorded. From each site the stratigraphy was taken into account; when possible, we collected pollen samples inside and outside the structures to compare airborne pollen deposited in the open with pollen transported into closed spaces. Pollen extraction included sieving and flotation that concentrated the grains even in sediments poor in organic matter.[6] Our aims were to analyse as many samples as we could to contribute to the understanding of the function of each site, while taking into account all the sites as constituent parts of the agrarian landscape of the region.[7] Samples of macroremains were systematically floated and sieved during the excavation. Macroremains, however, do not preserve well in calcareous/basic sediments and most of the results were obtained from pollen analyses.

Pollen was quite common with variable concentrations depending on its preservation and the presence of organic matter in the sediments. The floristic composition of pollen spectra gave good indications for the different uses of the sites. For example, plant diversity reflected the cultivation of cereal and legume crops.

The Case Studies of Case Nuove and San Martino

We discuss two sites taken as examples of the very different amounts and types of samples we studied from each site: Case Nuove and San Martino.[8]

Case Nuove was a small, open-air agro-processing point on a hilltop; there was a surface for foot-treading, a tank with a press, a deep well, and a dump of *dolia* remains.

Residue analyses indicated plant processing (tartaric and other acids in the *dolia;* possibly oil in the tank). Obtaining environmental data from the late Republican phase was hampered by the fact that no pollen could be collected from the use-phase layers due to the disturbance of the strata. Thus, the pollen information comes from a late antique rubbish pit representing only one phase (5th AD), whereas the macroremains and charcoal data come from both phases (1st BC and 5th AD). The landscape and woodland composition were characterised by a high diversity of species, corresponding to a fairly diverse environment with low forest cover. Pasture was a major part of the landscape around the site in late antiquity, but fields also were common. Among herb plants, cereals were the most significant, representing ca. 5% of the total pollen in the spectra. Pollen from cultivated woody plants was found in the late antique rubbish pit and included traces of *Olea, Vitis* and *Castanea.* Macroremains included also traces of *Juglans*-walnut, and some recordings of *Olea* and *Vitis.* The charcoal record, however, included only oak wood, and some unidentifiable charcoal fragments. This is in line with what one would expect, as olive trees and grapevines were prevalently exploited for fruits rather than for wood. The composition of cereals was quite varied and this is also evident from the macroremains, which point to a mixed cereal-producing regime: wheat species alternate or are grown alongside more drought-resistant types like barley.

Based on the pollen diagram and combining the botanical and archaeological evidence, and taking into account the geomorphology of the small hill, we concluded that the economic plants most likely were transported for processing to the top of Case Nuove. These plants prevalently consisted of cereals of different species, legumes, olives, and grapes. As the plant accumulations (pollen or fruits) found are limited, the amount of harvested yields transported to the top for processing will have been modest. There is evidence that the winnowing of cereals was practiced because the remains of chaff were found together with a high amount of pollen grains as discharge elements thrown in the late antique rubbish pit. We found that most land was devoted to pasture and that this practice was carried out through the entire use history of this site.

As cereals are processed in early summer and olive and grape fruits in autumn, the archaeobotanical evidence suggests that the site was used according to the seasons and their different agricultural harvests. Combining pollen, fungi, microcharcoal and plant macroremains, we assume that the farmers burnt any left-over rubbish and threw what remained in the pit to clean the site when processing activities were terminated. In fact, the majority of the macroremains, found in the top layer of the square pit, consisted of crop plants that were largely found charred. The place may have been periodically cleaned with small fires, but the fire cannot have been so prolonged as to destroy all the pollen in the deposit (as in fireplaces).

Very different from Case Nuove, San Martino was a small, single phase temporary or seasonal-use site. The structure's architecture suggests a modest investment consistent with a structure designed for sporadic use. The structure probably had a single pitched roof, possibly in straw. The house seems to have had no hearth, no water storage, and ceramics and fauna were extremely poor.

Pollen of cereals was present but not as abundant as at Case Nuove. Interestingly, we observed that the amount of cereal pollen was higher outside than inside the small structure. Present were also pollen and macroremains of legumes like *Hedysarum, Medicago, Melilotus* and *Trifolium,* which are fodder plants. The diversity of pasture-grazing plant species, which includes high values of Cichorieae pollen, suggests that pastures covered an important part of the landscape all around the site.

Therefore, the most definitive evidence for the site's function comes from the botanical data. The combined presence of pollen of Cichoriae and Fabaceae, the presence of coprophilous fungi and parasite eggs associated with herbivore dung all strongly point to the use of the structure for animal stabling. The considerable quantities of algae in this context may have been transported with the water they drunk. Given the size of the structure those animals would likely have been sheep and/or goats. On account of the strong presence of pasture, as well as the absence of other nearby structures, it seems likely the structure was used sporadically rather than as a permanent stable.

Concluding Remarks

The landscape of the area covered by the Roman Peasant Project was rich in different habitats and humans brought *in situ* plants here from diverse vegetation types and belts. Although each site is 'locally disturbed' because human activities strongly influenced the pollen spectra, we considered data from all the sites in combination to obtain a landscape reconstruction of the area based on a set of pollen sums referring to natural and human-induced environments.

The forest cover was low everywhere, and this suggests that the sites were located in open environments; the woodlands included conifer woods, oak woods, possibly mixed, and Mediterranean shrub lands. Such woodland was, however, located quite distant from the sites we discussed. Besides the oak-*Quercus* and beech-*Fagus* that we found in the form of charcoal and thus used as firewood and for building purposes, we also recorded a number of wild woody species that were used as a food resource, such as *Corylus, Cornus, Pistacia, Sambucus* and *Prunus.* The latter we counted as pollen in the samples.

Hygrophilous woods grew nearer to the sites, and we infer that wet environments were present everywhere. The landscape we are dealing with was a particularly groundwater rich area that proved both a benefit and a challenge. Sites may have been chosen to take advantage of local groundwater for agricultural purposes, and multiple perennial springs occuring in the area. However, this required careful draining and management as demonstrated by the need to dig a drain.

In the local human environments there were cereal fields and, as we saw, some plant processing occurred at Case Nuove and at other small sites in the area. Significant values of legumes suggest that some fields were cultivated for producing forage. Probably legumes rotated with cereals. The high amount of Cichorieae points both to the presence of pasturelands and to the presence of weeds developing in abandoned fields during the dry season (late summer). Among the other pollen taxa, in addition to evidence for plants of forests and grasslands, we found also evidence for many synanthropic and pasture-grazing plants. This suggests that dry pastures covered an important part of these lands, around and in the vicinity of the sites.

To conclude, according to the data produced from our interdisciplinary research and direct evidence from botany, the Roman sites recorded in the Roman Peasant Project were located in a landscape characterized by patches of fields and pastures. These were simultaneously present in an open and water-rich landscape that was intensively exploited and managed by peasant people who were skilled farmers.

Acknowledgements

We thank Kimberly Bowes and Emanuele Vaccaro for their invaluable support in sampling and studying the botanical record of the sites of the Roman Peasant Project. The results presented are part of research supported by the National Science Foundation under Grant BCS – 1063447. Further funding was provided by the University of Pennsylvania Museum of Archaeology and Anthropology, and the Loeb Classical Foundation. Eleonora Rattighieri carried out the palynological research as part of her PhD thesis (ESS School of University of Modena and Reggio Emilia). The archaeological sites with archaeobotanical data are included in the BRAIN database (brainplants.successoterra.net).

Notes

[1] Mercuri 2014; Mercuri et al. 2015.

[2] Bowes et al. 2011.

[3] Bowes et al. 2011.

[4] Bowes et al. 2017.

[5] Rattighieri et al. 2013; Bowes et al. 2015.

[6] Florenzano et al. 2012.

[7] Bowes et al. 2015.

[8] Bowes et al. 2015; Vaccaro et al. 2015; Mercuri et al. 2018.

References

Bowes et al. 2011

K. Bowes – M. Ghisleni – C. Grey – E. Vaccaro, Excavating the Roman Peasant, Expedition 53, 2011, 4–12.

Bowes et al. 2015

K. Bowes – A. M. Mercuri – E. Rattighieri – R. Rinaldi – A. Arnoldus-Huyzendveld – M. Ghisleni – C. Grey – M. MacKinnon – E. Vaccaro, Palaeoenvironment and Land-use of Roman Peasant Farmhouses in Southern Tuscany, Plant Biosystems 149, 2015, 174–184.

Bowes et al. 2017

K. Bowes – A. M. Mercuri – E. Rattighieri – R. Rinaldi – A. Arnoldus – Huyzendveld – M. Ghisleni, Peasant Agricultural Strategies in Southern Tuscany: Convertible Agriculture and the Importance of Pasture, in: T. C. A. de Haas – G. W. Tol (eds.), Rural Communities in a Globalizing Economy (Leiden 2017) 170–199.

Florenzano et al. 2012

A. Florenzano – A. M. Mercuri – A. Pederzoli – P. Torri – G. Bosi – L. Olmi – R. Rinaldi – M. Bandini Mazzanti, The Significance of Intestinal Parasite Remains in Pollen Samples from Mediaeval Pits in the Piazza Garibaldi of Parma, Emilia Romagna, Northern Italy, Geoarchaeology 27, 2012, 34–47.

Mercuri 2014

A. M. Mercuri, Genesis and Evolution of the Cultural Landscape in Central Mediterranean: the 'Where, When and How' through the Palynological Approach, Landscape Ecology 29, 2014, 1799–1810.

Mercuri et al. 2015

A. M. Mercuri – E. Allevato – D. Arobba – M. Bandini Mazzanti – G. Bosi – R. Caramiello – E. Castiglioni et al., Pollen and Macroremains from Holocene Archaeological Sites: a Dataset for the Understanding of the Biocultural Diversity of the Italian Landscape, RevPalaeobotPalynol 218, 2015, 250–266.

Mercuri et al. 2018

A. M. Mercuri – E. Rattighieri – R. Rinaldi – A. Florenzano – V. Vaccaro – K. Bowes, The Plant Landscape of Roman Tuscany and the Peasant Agricultural Strategies in the Cinigiano Area (central Italy), in: A. Florenzano – M. C. Montecchi – R. Rinaldi, Humans and Environmental Sustainability: Lessons from the Past Ecosystems of Europe and Northern Africa, 14th Conference of Environmental Archaeology, University of Modena and Reggio Emilia (Modena 2018) 166–167.

Rattighieri et al. 2013

E. Rattighieri – R. Rinaldi – A. M. Mercuri – K. Bowes, Land Use from Seasonal Archaeological Sites: the Archaeobotanical Evidence of Small Roman Farmhouses in Cinigiano, South-Eastern Tuscany – Central Italy, Annali di Botanica 3, 2013, 207–215.

Vaccaro et al. 2015

E. Vaccaro – M. Ghisleni – A. Arnoldus-Huyzendveld – C. Grey – K. Bowes, Excavating the Roman Peasant II: Excavations at Case Nuove, Cinigiano (GR), BAR 81, 2015, 129–179.

The Voice of the Silent Majority: Archaeological Surveys and the History of the Roman Countryside

Willem M. Jongman

The Roman Empire was and is a remarkable achievement in world history. At the height of its power it had a population that has been variously estimated at 60 to 100 million inhabitants, more than Han China at the time, and more than any Empire that had come before it. The Empire stretched from the bleak North of England to the Syrian Desert, and from Western Morocco to the Danube. For a while, population densities in many of the core regions were higher than ever before, and higher than they would be for a long time after. In addition, for a preindustrial society a remarkably high proportion of these people lived in cities, and often in really large cities.[1]

And yet, this was and remained an agricultural economy, where agriculture represented perhaps two thirds of GDP, and where 80% or more of the population lived in the countryside and worked in agriculture. For all its potential achievements, the Roman economy was not a modern economy.

Those modern economies are characterized by sustained real growth of per capita incomes of at least 1% per year, and often more. Aggregate growth is usually even rather more, because modern societies also experienced significant population increases. By contrast, preindustrial economies are characterized by only low per capita growth at best. In fact, the most common pattern is that of a negative correlation between trends in population and trends in incomes. Income growth could often not keep up with population growth. Periods of population growth experienced declining labour incomes, until Malthusian positive checks would turn the tide with wars, epidemics and famines.[2] After such periods of catastrophic mortality, labour would become scarce and hence was only used where its marginal productivity was highest. Therefore, after demographic crises labour incomes would be rather higher, as was most clearly demonstrated after the Black Death of the 14th century.[3] Conversely, land had become relatively more abundant, so land values and rents were lower. Between them, these two developments of higher wages and lower rents reduced income inequality between workers and landowners.

Historical reconstructions of the medieval and early modern rural economy have thus moved between concerns about historical change on the one hand, and the strength of a Malthusian ceiling on the other hand.[4] The preindustrial economy was by no means static, but could it also escape from its Malthusian constraints, and experience real economic growth where both population and standard of living would increase? The logic of the pessimistic Malthusian model is impeccable, and there is historical corroboration from mediaeval and early modern European history. At the same time at least the early modern Netherlands and England experienced both population growth and improving standards of living.[5] So we must ask ourselves what scenario applied to the Roman experience. Can survey archaeology contribute to an answer?

The first central variable for such analysis is of course population, as it is the numerator in many equations. What was the trend in aggregate population numbers, was it the same all over the Empire, and how can we know this? Until quite recently discussion of such population trends was mostly concerned with competing interpretations of the census numbers for Republican Italy. Unfortunately, these census figures only exist for two centuries, and only for Italy. To make matters worse, there is significant scholarly disagreement about who were counted in these censuses.[6] Therefore, in my view the census numbers are not very helpful.[7] A recent alternative has been to use field survey data to reconstruct rural population trends. Lisa Fentress' pioneering work has shown that by assigning estimated population numbers to the different site types we can estimate total population for a region. Absolute numbers are inevitably quite insecure, but relative changes over time should be far more robust. At this moment, reconstructions of long term demographic trends from survey data are still few in number, particularly outside Italy. However, a tentative hypothesis may be formulated that population in Italy increased during the later Republican period, and started to decline again quite dramatically from perhaps the later 2nd century AD, even if regional differences in magnitude and timing are important, and deserve concerted investigation.[8]

Beyond trends in population, such analyses from settlement data can also show changes in the relative proportions of people on small versus large estates and social relations in the countryside. Therefore, such data are directly relevant for classic and important debates about the decline of the small farmer in Italy in the later Republic, or the growth of large estates in Late Antiquity. Theoretically, a growth in population in the earlier period should have depressed marginal labour productivity and hence labour incomes and improved the marginal productivity of the land and hence increased land prices and rents. Socially, the most likely result would be a decline of the small peasant and the growth of large estates. And indeed, this is of course the traditional narrative, even if the explanation is usually an entirely different one, and based on a presumed decline in population rather than on demographic pressure, and connected to the rise of slavery in agriculture and the migration of impoverished peasants to the city and to Rome in particular.[9] However, *ceteris paribus* such demographic contraction should have improved labour productivity and labour incomes, and should have depressed rents and hence elite incomes. In short, the traditional interpretations of late Republican and late Imperial economy and society do not sit easily with the standard economic analysis of the consequences of changes in factor proportions by shifts along the production function.

This is not to say that such an alternative non-Malthusian scenario is impossible, but it would imply that rather than a shift along the production function, there was a shift of the production function itself, where the same quantities of factors of production produced more or less than before (i.e. real growth and decline). So what actually happened, and can survey archaeology help? For Italy, the archaeological picture seems to be quite clear that there was population growth and urban growth in the Republican period and that there was a growth of, first, larger farms and later really large estates.[10] At the same time, however, the new picture that has emerged from survey archaeology is that in many areas the small farmer continued to be a major part of the rural landscape. The literary picture of a landscape devoid of small farmers and dominated by large estates worked only by slaves is a misleading one. Villa agriculture came on top of continued peasant farming.

Explanations for this growth in population have shifted in recent years. When originally this was viewed as part of Roman military expansion, Terrenato and others have demonstrated that the same expansion occurred not just in Roman controlled territory, but also outside the sphere of Roman influence, or before Roman conquest. It would seem to be part of a much wider Mediterranean phenomenon, of which Roman demographic expansion itself was a product rather than a cause.[11] If demographic expansion and urbanization were part of a Mediterranean-wide process, trade and market integration become an important vector for convergence and regional connectivity. And indeed, the penetration of long-distance trade beyond urban centres and into the countryside has become an important issue.[12] Here, archaeological surveys have a lot to contribute. What is also remarkable is the greater reach of long distance trade, into, for example the Red Sea and the Indian Ocean, or along the African Coast.[13] Some have even suggested tentatively that the convergence of many such trends may have been part of a global development that also included, for example, Han China, and that owed much to a period of increasingly favourable climate.[14]

Similar issues emerge when we ponder the causes and consequences of the late antique demographic contraction. Again, assuming for the moment that there was indeed such a contraction, the *ceteris paribus* prediction would be that marginal labour productivity increased and hence labour incomes, and that the marginal productivity of the land deteriorated, and that hence rents declined. Therefore, the model predicts that small farmers would do better, and that big landowners would see their position eroded. Late antiquity should be a world of happy and prosperous peasant farmers, and lower rent income for the landowning elite. Again, the question remains, if this is what happened; it certainly deviates from the quite commonly held view that labour in late antiquity became increasingly oppressed, and that big magnates and their large estates became more prominent.

And indeed, the late antique transformation does involve discussions of demographic contraction, urban decline, rural social change and new productive strategies, but also of stagnation in shipping and long distance trade, and a return to more local wares.[15] An explanation of why this contraction did not benefit labour incomes would then have to come from three potential developments. The first is a shift of the production function because of unfavourable climate change: the same quantities of land and labour produced less. The second would be that urban decline reduced the beneficial division of labour between town and country, and reduced the potential for profitable market crops.[16] The third would be the growth of oppression to counter the forces of the labour market.[17]

Survey archaeology can contribute a lot to all of these important questions. Assuming that the hypothesis of demographic growth and subsequent contraction is indeed confirmed, we want to know if this population growth did indeed depress the standard of living and if the decline of late antique population improved the standard of living. Alternatively, did Roman population grow because of increased prosperity, and declined because of increased poverty (i.e. that there was indeed a shift of the production function itself)? To put it another way, was the standard of living the dependent variable or the independent variable? And, of course, there is the empirical question how we can reconstruct such changes in standard of living. So, what was the ratio between estimated population numbers and quantities of artefacts of various types, and how did this change over time? Here, so-called high income elasticity goods have a central place, which are goods that are in disproportionally greater demand if incomes rise (and disproportionally less when incomes decline). When incomes rise, people will not increase their consumption of subsistence (low income elasticity) foods by much, if at all (in fact, they may even reduce their consumption of such goods). They will spend the extra income on more luxurious (high income elasticity) foods such as meat or fruits, and the better and more expensive consumer goods such as fine table ware. Therefore, increases in the per capita consumption of high income elasticity goods are an excellent tracer of increases in incomes, even if we do not have direct evidence for incomes. Archaeologically, such consumer spending can be quite visible, in terms of volume, but also in terms of changing proportions of (low income elasticity) coarse ware versus (high income elasticity) fine ware. The same is true for changes over time in the proportion between local wares and imported wares: what does that tell us about purchasing power, but also about market integration and cultural identity?

Yet, for all the optimism about the analytical potential of archaeological surveys, it is important to realize its current limitations as well. The first of these is that the relation between what we find on the surface and what was really underneath can be quite surprising. In particular, what may seem to be surface traces of a farm may well turn out to be something quite different once we actually excavate. Here, the Roman Peasant Project has been a pioneering contribution that deserves to be followed by many more such projects.[18] Methodologically, all locations on the spectrum of extensive survey to intensive survey, to hyper-intensive survey and geophysics, and all the way to small actual excavations deserve to be represented and strategically combined if we want to get maximum information and understanding from a minimum of effort.

A second area where much more is possible is showcased here in the archaeobotanical paper by Mercuri et al. We should never forget that agriculture was the principal rural economic activity; by and large archaeobotany and archaeozoology are the principal tools to retrieve data on that, and to reconstruct shifts in agricultural strategies to respond to changing circumstances.[19]

A third area is that of obstacles to generalization. By now we have quite a few survey datasets for Italy, and also for some other regions of the Empire. Unfortunately little has been done to integrate the results of these many surveys. Often, archaeologists have insisted on the uniqueness of their own survey, and explanations were often based on the unique local geography. Generalization was usually avoided, and was not made any easier because projects insisted on their own superior methodologies, and kept the underlying datasets inaccessible to other researchers. As a result, the potential of these massive datasets was rarely used in larger historical reconstructions. When they were used, this had to be done with analyses that could not be based on the underlying data.[20] Collins-Elliot (this volume) proposes one – mathematical – way to analyse these data on a more aggregate level. Alternatively, the recent Roman Hinterland Project, integrating the three major survey datasets around the city of Rome, is a first example of what can be achieved when teams join forces and homogenize and integrate their datasets.[21] It allows for far more secure identification of the major trends, but also for more secure identification of local deviations from that trend. We can only know what is specific to the local, and why, if we can compare it to the global.[22]

In conclusion, I would argue that the big story of Roman economic and social change is not only one of its fascinating urban economy, but also that of rural population, production, standard of living and social relations. Survey archaeology is our best bet to study these developments, but all the more so if we make some important strategic decisions to get as much out of these data as we can, to write local histories, but also to write the big story of the Empire at large. Finally, to understand the meaning of what we observe, we need to be aware of the economic logic of the situation, and join the comparative historical debates of pre-industrial economies and societies. The Roman case is almost uniquely interesting for its achievements and ultimate failure.

Notes

[1] Hanson 2016.

[2] Jongman 2012; 2014.

[3] Campbell 2016.

[4] Clark 2007.

[5] De Vries – Van der Woude 1997; Broadberry et al. 2015.

[6] Scheidel 2007.

[7] Jongman 2009.

[8] Launaro 2011; Fentress 2009; De Haas et al. 2011; Jongman 2009.

[9] Hopkins 1978.

[10] e.g. Carandini et al. 2002; Terrenato 2012; De Haas et al. 2011.

[11] Terrenato 2012; Launaro 2011; Knust this volume.
[12] Launaro this volume; Schörner and Schreck this volume.
[13] Nappo 2018.
[14] Knust, this volume; Jongman 2012; Jongman 2014.
[15] Duncan-Jones 2004; Harper 2016.
[16] Jongman 2016.
[17] Jongman 2014; c.f. Brenner 1976; Borsch 2005; Acemoglu – Robinson 2012.
[18] Bowes et al. 2011.
[19] Bowes et al. 2017.
[20] Ikeguchi 2007; Launaro 2011.
[21] Attema et al. this volume.
[22] Knust, this volume.

References

Acemoglu – Robinson 2012
D. Acemoglu – A. Robinson, Why Nations Fail. The Origins of Power, Prosperity, and Poverty (New York 2012).

Attema et al. (this volume)
P. Attema – T. de Haas – G. Tol – J. Seubers, Towards an Integrated Database for the Study of Long-term Settlement Dynamics, Economic Performance and Demography in the Pontine Region and the Hinterland of Rome.

Borsch 2005
S. J. Borsch, The Black Death in Egypt and England. A Comparative Study (Austin 2005).

Bowes et al. 2011
K. Bowes – M. Ghisleni – C. Grey – E. Vaccaro, Excavating the Roman Peasant, Expedition 53, 2011, 4–12.

Bowes et al. 2017
K. Bowes – A. M. Mercuri – E. Rattighieri – R. Rinaldi – A. Arnoldus-Huyzendveld – M. Ghisleni, Peasant Agricultural Strategies in Southern Tuscany: Convertible Agriculture and the Importance of Pasture, in: T. de Haas – G. W. Tol (eds.), Rural Communities in a Globalizing Economy (Leiden 2017) 170–199.

Brenner 1976
R. Brenner, Agrarian Class Structure and Economic Development in Pre-industrial Europe, Past and Present 70, 1976, 30–75.

Broadberry et al. 2015
S. Broadberry – B. M. S. Campbell – A. Klein – M. Overton – B. Van Leeuwen, British Economic Growth 1270–1870 (Cambridge 2015).

Campbell 2016
B. Campbell, The Great Transition: Climate, Disease and Society in the Late-medieval World (Cambridge 2016).
Carandini et al. 2002
A. Carandini – M. Celuzza – E. Fentress – I. Attolini (eds.), Paesaggi d'Etruria. Valle dell'Albegna, Valle d'Oro, Valle del Chiarone, Valle del Tafone (Rome 2002).
Clark 2007
G. Clark, A Farewell to Alms. A Brief Economic History of the World (Princeton 2007).
Collins-Elliot (this volume)
S. A. Collins-Elliot, Measuring Rural Economic Development through Categorical Data Analysis in Southern Etruria and Latium (400 BCE–50 CE).
De Haas et al. 2011
T. De Haas – G. Tol – P. Attema, Investing in the Colonia and Ager of Antium, Facta 5, 2011, 111–144.
De Vries – Van der Woude 1997
J. De Vries – A. M. Van der Woude, The First Modern Economy: Success, Failure and Perseverance of the Dutch Economy 1500–1815 (Cambridge 1997).
Duncan-Jones 2004
R. Duncan-Jones, Economic Change and the Transition to Late Antiquity, in: S. Swain – M. Edwards (eds.), Approaching Late Antiquity. The Transformation from Early to Late Empire (Oxford 2004) 20–52.
Fentress 2009
E. Fentress, Peopling the Countryside: Roman Demography in the Albegna Valley and Jerba, in: A. Bowman – A. Wilson (eds.), Quantifying the Roman Economy: Methods and Problems (Oxford 2009) 127–161.
Hanson 2016
J. W. Hanson, An Urban Geography of the Roman World, 100 B.C. to A.D. 300. (Oxford 2016).
Harper 2017
K. Harper, The Fate of Rome. Climate, Disease and the End of an Empire (Princeton 2017).
Hopkins 1978
K. Hopkins, Conquerors and Slaves (Cambridge 1978).
Ikeguchi 2007
M. Ikeguchi, A Method for Interpreting and Comparing Field Survey Data, in: P. Bang – M. Ikeguchi – H. Ziche (eds.) Ancient Economies and Modern Methodologies (Bari 2007) 137–158.
Jongman 2009
W. M. Jongman, Archaeology, Demography and Roman Economic Growth, in: A. Bowman – A. Wilson (eds.), Quantifying the Roman Economy: Methods and Problems (Oxford 2009) 115–126.
Jongman 2012
W. M. Jongman, Roman Economic Change and the Antonine Plague: Endogenous, Exogenous, or What?, in: E. Lo Cascio (ed.), L'impatto della peste Antonina (Bari 2012) 253–263.

Jongman 2014
W. M. Jongman, Re-constructing the Roman Economy, in: L. Neal – J. Williamson (eds.), The Cambridge History of Capitalism 1 (Cambridge 2014) 75–100.

Jongman 2016
W. M. Jongman, Italian Urbanization and Roman Economic Growth, in: L. Capogrossi Colognesi – E. Lo Cascio – E. Tassi Scandone (eds.), L'Italia dei Flavi. Atti del Convegno, Roma, 4–5 Ottobre 2012 (Rome 2016) 105–117.

Knust (this volume)
J. E. M. Knust, Far from the Walls. Explaining Rural Settlement Dispersal within Roman, Mediterranean and Global Frameworks.

Launaro 2011
A. Launaro, Peasants and Slaves: the Rural Population of Italy (200 B.C. to A.D. 100) (Cambridge 2011).

Launaro (this volume)
A. Launaro, A View from the Margins: Interamna Lirenas and Its Territory in the Long Term.

Mercuri et al. (this volume)
A. M. Mercuri – E. Rattighieri – R. Rinaldi – A. Florenzano, The Archaeobotanical Study of Agriculture of Roman Peasants: Skilled Farmers of the 1st BC–5th AD in Tuscany, Central Italy.

Nappo 2018
D. Nappo, I Porti Romani nel Mar Rosso da Augusto al Tardoantico (Naples 2018).

Scheidel 2007
W. Scheidel, Demography, in: W. Scheidel – I. Morris – R. P. Saller (eds.) The Cambridge Economic History of the Greco-Roman World (Cambridge 2007) 38–86.

Schörner – Schreck (this volume)
G. Schörner – V. Schreck, Production and Trade in Late Republican and Imperial Inland Etruria: Integrating Archaeological and Archaeometric Results of the Val di Pesa and Val Orme-Project

Terrenato 2012
N. Terrenato, The Essential Countryside: the Roman World, in: S. E. Alcock – R. Osborne, Classical Archaeology ²(Chichester, MA 2012).

Printing and Binding
Books on Demand GmbH, Norderstedt